# The Repetitive
# Beat Generation

**STEVE REDHEAD** is Professor of Law and Popular Culture at the Manchester Metropolitan University. He is author of *Sing When You're Winning, The End-of-the-Century Party, Football With Attitude, Unpopular Cultures, Subculture to Clubcultures* and *Post-Fandom and the Millennial Blues* and editor of *Rave Off, The Passion and The Fashion* and *The Clubcultures Reader.* He lives in Manchester.

# Repetitive
# **Beat**Generation

## Steve Redhead

*REBEL*
inc.

First published in Great Britain in 2000 by
Rebel Inc, an imprint of
Canongate Books Ltd, 14 High Street,
Edinburgh EH1 1TE

10 9 8 7 6 5 4 3 2 1

Rebel Inc series editor: Kevin Williamson
www.rebelinc.net

*British Library Cataloguing-in-Publication Data*
A catalogue record for this book is available on
request from the British Library

ISBN 0 86241 930 1

Typeset by Palimpsest Book Production Limited,
Polmont, Stirlingshire
Printed and bound by
Creative Print and Design, Ebbw Vale, Wales.

This book is dedicated to Sheila Brown,
my daughters Laura and Ellie Redhead
and my parents Geoff and Jean Redhead

# Contents

# Acknowledgements

Rebel Inc/Canongate, and especially Kevin Williamson, for their faith.

Appreciation to Craig Wood of In Demand Recordings for his help in getting things started.

Many thanks to Irvine Welsh, Nicholas Blincoe, Jeff Noon, Hanif Kureishi, Douglas Rushkoff, Sarah Champion, Kevin Williamson, John King, Jamie Macdonald, Toni Davidson, Gordon Legge, Roddy Doyle, John Sutton, Jon Savage, Donal Scannell, Simon Frith, Alan Warner, Duncan McLean, Emer Martin, Q, Courttia Newland, Elaine Palmer, Michael McLoughlin, Mike McCormack, Laura Hird, Geoff Dyer, Simon Prosser, Mark Perryman, Dave Haslam and Andrew Ward for their time, hospitality, interest, conversation and correspondence.

Thanks to all my colleagues at the Manchester Metropolitan University who read interview transcripts and made helpful suggestions.

# Introduction
## The Repetitive Beat Generation - Live

## Introduction to the 90s New Fiction

Armed with a tape recorder and a bagful of 90s fiction, CDs and a Sony discman I travelled Britain and Ireland in search of the repetitive beat generation, my less than serious moniker for the mostly male twenty and thirtysomething cult fiction writers who have challenged the literary establishment with a new, counter cultural attitude. When I returned from my journeys I plugged in my personal computer and e-mailed those I had missed on my various travels. The writers told me their stories in a variety of places – bars, flats, theatres, coffee/café bars, cyberspace – and reflected on their personal and cultural histories, the battles for recognition and the myriad literary, political and cultural influences on their writing. They were enthusiastic, generous with their time and extremely modest considering what has been achieved so far against difficult odds. This book is their story, told in their own words.

Back in 1992 Elizabeth Young and Graham Caveney published a book, *Shopping In Space*, on contemporary New York fiction, subtitled *Essays on American Blank Generation Fiction*. Interesting though it was, Young and Caveney's book concentrated on writers like Jay McInerney and Bret Easton Ellis who were then cemented to the late 70s and 80s US attitudes, lifestyles and music. In 1992 there seemed little overt sign that a literary movement containing largely younger writers on the other side of the Atlantic in Britain and Ireland might flourish sufficiently to reflect the changing culture of the last decade of the century.

Douglas Coupland – straight outta Vancouver – had begun to make an international impact with his novel *Generation X*, published the previous year in the USA, whilst writers like Dennis Cooper and Gary Indiana were still ploughing a lonely furrow in American gay splatter. But apart from the early beginnings of someone like Roddy Doyle in Dublin, or Martin Millar in Brixton, in the late 80s there was little in terms of published fiction which would lead anyone to predict what has since unfolded. Then, miraculously, apparently out of nowhere in 1993 Secker and Warburg published Irvine Welsh's first novel *Trainspotting* – following Welsh and a number of other authors' emergence in the Scottish litzine (literary fanzine) world of Rebel Inc and Clocktower Press. What has been mislabelled ever since as litpop, Britlit or Britpulp was on its way as an unfolding media event.

Soon, authors' personal appearances in bookshops like Waterstone's or Dillon's sold out in the same time as concert tickets. Virgin and HMV record chains sold shrink-wrapped copies of the books by the truckload alongside the usual fare of t-shirts, videos, CDs, tapes and 12″ vinyl records. Readings in nightclubs – venues more used to pounding drum and bass, trip hop and speed garage – by repetitive beat generation writers started to become commonplace.

Rebel Inc, the magazine which had helped to start the whole genre in the first place, published two successful anthologies of novellas as an imprint of Canongate Books: *Children of Albion Rovers* and *Rovers Return*, along with free pocket sized 'samplers' of its rapidly growing fiction list. First published – then banned – in 1996, *Children of Albion Rovers* was marketed with packs of football cards of the authors and a huge nightclub event, 1,000 tickets sold out, with Irvine Welsh, Paul Reekie, three sound systems and an underground cinema.

Kevin Williamson had begun putting together the first *Rovers* anthology in 1994, the same year that Toni Davidson started working on a collection of contemporary 'stimulant-based writing', which eventually came out as a Serpent's Tail paperback called *Intoxication*. Meanwhile, Sarah Champion anthologised short stories in 1997 about Ecstasy culture in *Disco Biscuits*, a book which *i-D* magazine described as a 'publishing phenomenon'. *Disco 2000*, an end-of-the-millennium follow up, soon emerged, with anthologies of Irish 'fresh fiction' and twisted 'travel fiction' not far behind. The first two were accompanied by compilation CDs of appropriate dance tracks.

# The Phenomenon of Irvine Welsh and *Trainspotting*

Beneath this sudden explosion of media focus though there was always the story of the writers themselves and how a literary underground became overground in the rapidly accelerating global culture at the end of the millennium. None of this tale was really told properly. There were plenty of snide comments from a literary and media establishment who didn't like the way that the system was being bucked by a bunch of outsiders (Kevin Williamson described it in *Dazed and Confused* as an 'assault') and often built up the writers as 'stars' only to gleefully knock them down soon afterwards. Enter Irvine Welsh.

*Trainspotting*, ostensibly, is the story of Mark Renton and his friends Spud, Sick Boy, Tommy and the rest of the underbelly of 80s Edinburgh junk culture. This is not a Scottish William Burroughs parody. Americans of the beat generation, or, for that matter, the later blank generation, would have difficulty making any meaningful comparisons. By the time the film of the book crossed the Atlantic in 1996 a large part of the dialogue was redubbed because of fears that American audiences would be unable to understand the supposedly 'heavy' Edinburgh accents of Robert Carlyle, Ewan McGregor and the rest of the cast (including Welsh himself as a drug dealer in a cameo role). The *Paris Review* magazine even produced a glossary to assist overseas readers of Irvine Welsh: for example 'coffin dodger' (senior citizen), 'collies' (drugs) and 'biscuit-ersed' (self-pitying) were all explained in an issue in 1996.

*Trainspotting*, the film, made by the team who put together the successful 90s low budget Scottish film *Shallow Grave* – Danny Boyle as director, Andrew MacDonald as producer and John Hodge as screenwriter – has grossed in excess of £42 million (not bad for a £1.6 million initial investment) and made Irvine Welsh a global household name. Its brilliant soundtrack featured dance music pioneers like Leftfield, Underworld and Primal Scream, contemporary pop like Blur, Elastica and Sleeper, alongside rock classics from Lou Reed and

Iggy Pop. A follow up album *Trainspotting 2* was eventually released with the rest of the film soundtrack plus some remixes. Ironically, Irvine Welsh himself has had a follow up – *Trainspotting 2* – novel project for some time but has held on to it for possible future use preferring at the time to write *Marabou Stork Nightmares* which 'seemed a more interesting thing to do rather than retread'. Irvine Welsh talking about *Trainspotting* in the conversation in this book is still an author pleasantly surprised by its astounding literary, cultural and commercial success throughout the world.

In some ways Irvine Welsh, and to some extent other new Scottish writers too, come from within a 'Celtic story-telling tradition' which marks them out from others included in the repetitive beat generation category. Welsh concedes that 'there is a lot of bad stuff' in repetitive beat, and especially 'chemical' generation fiction but he argues that 'there's a lot of bad stuff in other areas' of fiction which never attracts anything like the same adverse comment. Point taken.

The written word of Irvine Welsh has 'bled' into various other forms. Apart from *Trainspotting*, three stories from *The Acid House* – 'A Soft Touch', 'The Acid House' and 'Granton Star Cause' (with, originally, enough good music soundtrack material to fill two albums including Oasis and Chemical Brothers tracks alongside a host of lesser knowns) were combined as *The Acid House* movie. In addition the novella *A Smart Cunt* and the first two stories from *Ecstasy* have all been scheduled to be filmed. For Alex Usborne and Paul McGuigan's *The Acid House*, which was released in 1998, Welsh himself was co-opted to write the screenplay. Welsh's first stage play *You'll Have Had Your Hole*, which premiered in Leeds at the West Yorkshire Play House, was being touted by production companies as a possible film even before the opening night. Following on from 'Big Man' Welsh's spoken word collaboration with Primal Scream and legendary dub producer Adrian Sherwood for the Euro '96 soccer tournament in England (an X-rated 'Scotland' single released for a few days only by Creation under the rubrik Big Man and the Scream Team Meet the Barmy Army Uptown), the 1998 *Rock The Dock* compilation in support of the Liverpool Dockers had Welsh's spoken word introduction to the nature of the dispute, which was also given widespread publicity by Liverpool footballer Robbie Fowler's t-shirt protest. Shortly after the end of the strike the film *Dockers* was screened on Channel Four with Welsh and Jimmy McGovern listed as two of the contributors.

Irvine Welsh's home town team, Hibernian FC, gave the name to his band Hibee-Nation. Along with Henry Cullen, Sarah Jane Harrison and Kris Needs, former editor of one of the oldest music fanzines *Zigzag* (begun in 1969), he put out disco influenced dance records like 'The Key To The House of Love (Gies It)' and '(I Sentence You To A) Life of Dance'. Welsh's own commitment to DJ culture has been long standing but fame allowed him to indulge his passion for the decks. He has DJ-ed at clubs like Back To Basics in Leeds and Bugged Out at Sankey's Soap in Manchester as well as in Cannes and Ibiza and been interviewed and featured in dance culture magazines like *Wax*. His film and theatre work is underscored by all sorts of popular music culture references.

Welsh points out that in the early 90s in Edinburgh writers and performers tried all sorts of ways to get the written and spoken word across in new contexts, sometimes simply having readings at clubs or else trying drum machines, DJ backing or other musical accompaniment. Performance poetry was significant in this context and in an echo of both beat generation readings and post-punk poets like John Cooper Clarke, Seething Wells and Attila the Stockbroker.

Fiction writers from other traditions – Martin Amis or James Kelman – were writers to react against in some ways rather than direct influences on the new 90s fiction. Welsh certainly reacted against Amis' *London Fields* for instance but he insists that does not mean he disliked such authors *per se*. James Kelman's pioneering writing often came up in my various conversations with the new fiction writers.

Welsh says his inspiration for writing is not really drug culture at all but 'working-class culture' in general. He contrasts this with the increasingly powerful self-referential media culture, arguing that for example the mass media highlights someone like Julie Burchill whereas the culture 'outside' of the media – the fans – would instead revere a performer like John Lydon (Johnny Rotten of the Sex Pistols) rather than a celebrity journalist. The media, with its barely contained smugness when reporting Welsh's occasional binges or disdain when haranguing him for commenting on books he has been sent to read by publishers, has played a strangely contradictory role in the making of the phenomenon of Irvine Welsh.


## The Social and Political Backdrop to the New Fiction

For me, the book's title of *The Repetitive Beat Generation* was born with the then Tory government's coining of the term 'repetitive beats' in the bizarre drafting of its Criminal Justice and Public Order Bill. Aimed at a particular dimension of dance music culture, and its coming together with the anti-materialism of new age travellers in the early 90s, this draconian Act, on the statute book since 1994, symbolically outlawed a whole generation which had since the late 80s 'fought the law' – and nearly won – in establishing a new underground culture of music, drugs and lifestyle which eventually became mainstream as corporate 'clubculture' by the mid to late 90s.

It is a fact, though, that the repetitive beat generation writers were expressing in fiction everything which was new. In a supposedly post-literate culture where video, TV and other image-dominated technologies prevail, and where traditional publishing values still rule when it comes to the written word, new fiction can be said to gaining in popularity. In an age where use of the internet is expanding rapidly and where print remixes appear of virtual novels first written in cyberspace, a new wave of fiction has caught the imagination of a generation under 35. Youth culture, or counter culture, fiction of the 90s emerged at exactly the same time that countries like Britain cracked down on 'uncultured youth' or, in the authorities' eyes, unruly youth culture. States in various countries actually took umbrage at libertarian youth culture which had emerged at the end of the 80s, a decade dominated by New Right thinking and the scene of free market social and economic experiments.

This book playfully, yet seriously, recalls 'angelheaded hipster' Jack Kerouac's famous phrase 'the beat generation' but its actual title is taken directly from the text of the Criminal Justice and Public Order Act 1994, a statute introduced by the post-Thatcher government of John Major which notoriously sought to 'criminalise' a whole youth culture. Section 63 (1) (b) of the Act defines its target as music with 'sounds wholly or predominantly characterised by the emission of a succession of repetitive beats'.

From the mid-80s in Britain until the present day a generational change occurred in popular music and culture completely unheralded in the early 80s. The Chronology in this book (p.163) gives a rough guide to this period, from around 1987 to the present. These years provide the social and political backdrop to the new fiction. The culture of freedom to choose (brilliantly sent up in *Trainspotting*) which was promoted in these times only extended so far however: legal and other forms of discipline and regulation were coming up around the bend.

## The Shifts in Popular Culture

The areas of popular culture most spectacularly subjected to legal intervention in the last decade or so have been recreational drug culture and football fandom. The law on illegal drugs, the Misuse of Drugs Act 1971, pre-dated the emergence of large scale use of Ecstasy from the mid-80s, when, together with amphetamines, cannabis, cocaine and other variants, hundreds of thousands of young people regularly chose to breach the prevailing criminal law. For a time such cultural change mellowed out the football stands and terraces, too, and laws introduced ostensibly to curb macho 'hooliganism', the Football Spectators Act 1989 and the Football (Offences) Act 1990, had less effect than the illegal substances consumed days before the match in nightclubs.

Irvine Welsh's *Marabou Stork Nightmares* is a disturbing novel in which he gives more space than in any of his other books to soccer casuals. A whole new football fan literature followed later in the 90s

– very different to the lineage begun by Nick Hornby's *Fever Pitch* – when Welsh's publishers Jonathan Cape launched John King's loose football-fiction trilogy *The Football Factory*, *Headhunters* and *England Away*. Cape also recruited the former manager of legendary scouse band The Farm (who in the early 80s started their own football and music fanzine *The End*) as a fiction writer on football and music. *Awaydays*, Kevin Sampson's debut, is the story of Tranmere Rovers' casuals in 1979 where in 'Birkenhead, Merseyside, smack and Maggie Thatcher are still less of an issue than Lois jeans and Adidas Forest Hill training shoes'. Welsh was inevitably sent these novels to read before they were published. His assessment of King's *The Football Factory* was emblazoned on the front cover: 'the best book I've ever read about football and working-class culture in the nineties. Buy, steal or borrow a copy now'. Pulp Books soon put out Mick Bower's *Football Seasons*, a novel about Sheffield, gay culture masculinity and modern football.

Kevin Sampson, himself a lifelong Liverpool supporter, is as ambivalent as the other repetitive beat generation authors about the way that New Football has come to represent some of these wider cultural changes of de-industrialisation, globalisation and media-induced embourgeoisement. In *Extra Time*, his diary of the 1997–1998 football season following his team home and away published by Jonathan Cape's sports imprint Yellow Jersey, he notes: 'What . . . we have to ask ourselves is whether we want to carry on mourning, moaning and dragging our heels or whether we can embrace the new face of New Football. Can we just accept that we've been part of something fantastic, but now it's time to put the memories in the scrapbook and get on with the new reality? Can we sit next to guys and gals in football shirts with radios stuck to their ears, all part of one big, happy, football family?' The excavation of working-class football history also led Irvine Welsh to write the foreword and the TV screenplay for Phil Vasili's history of Britain's first black footballer from the beginning of the century, Arthur Wharton.

For Donald Dewar, First Minister in the new Scottish Parliament, the writing in the new fiction itself – particularly in the way he sees it as derived from authors such as James Kelman – tends towards 'workerism'. Ironically, the label Britlit which the media used to cover the fiction success stories of authors as diverse as Irvine Welsh, Nick Hornby, Alan Warner and Martin Amis helped to link Welsh and others with the New Labour era because of the earlier linking of Britpop, another spurious stereotype, to Tony Blair and the creation of a post-New Right era. The *New Statesman*, for instance, forthrightly included short stories by Irvine Welsh and Alan Warner in its General Election victory special in May 1997.

In fact Irvine Welsh had always spoken critically of New Labour, criticising Labour's history of (in his view) implementing Tory policies. Introducing playscripts of his works *Trainspotting* and pre-club night *Headstate* Welsh argued: '"Tory misrule" or "monetarism" or "Thatcherism" . . . all these things actually started in 1976, not 1979, when the Labour Government expressly went to the institutions of multi-national capitalism with a programme for the domestic economy based on those principles. Now, under Blair's leadership, they seem set to carry them forward with renewed vigour as the Tories have run out of steam.'

New Labour itself has been criticised for laddish tendencies, especially by Helen Wilkinson of the Demos think tank, but the 'men behaving badly' new lad culture has also been seen by some as part of the reason for the commercial success of the repetitive beat generation writers such as John King and Irvine Welsh. Welsh wrote a column for *Loaded* magazine (because they asked him, he says), the epitome of new laddism as far as some critics are concerned. It is noticeable that Laura Hird − one of six authors (five male) collected in the first of the anthologies by Rebel Inc's Kevin Williamson − was for John King (a definite Laura Hird fan) 'like a male writer' and that Sarah Champion as editor was in *Disco Biscuits* promoting no less than nineteen stories by various male authors. Nevertheless, *Shenanigans*, featuring outstanding women writers like Emer Martin (also in the second Rebel Inc collection) restored the balance somewhat as well as showcasing relative newcomers like Mike McCormack. All the writers I interviewed were as interested in promoting female writers as male; gay as well as straight. They were united in putting out the best possible fiction and short stories at any one time.

Writers such as Irvine Welsh and Alan Warner have also been accused by critics of stereotyping in their portrayal of female characters. Nevertheless the fiction of the repetitive beat generation has more often put masculinity up on trial – either that of the authors themselves or the culture of masculinities they often write about. Additionally, Warner's *Sopranos* novel has been praised for its portrayal of grrrl culture. For Jeremy Gilbert, writing in a series of essays on *The Modernisers' Dilemma* in 'The Age of Blair': 'even the fiction of Chemical Generation hero Irvine Welsh – peopled as it is by lads, hard-men, schemies and casuals – almost always ends up endorsing a feminist/feminised perspective (a rapist is castrated, a casual dies for love, a chauvinist café customer gets a used tampon in his soup) while offering sophisticated and reflexive considerations of the status of post-industrial masculinity. Indeed. Welsh's mediations on consumption, hedonism and contemporary maculinity ("I think I'll stick to drugs to get me through the long, dark night of late capitalism . . ." muses one character about his non-identification with socialist politics) can be read almost as a counter-discourse to the simplicities of New Laddism. It's no accident that Welsh – who actually writes as much about soccer hooligans as about Ecstasy – has been so firmly identified with rave culture.' Writers like Nicholas Blincoe and Toni Davidson explicitly explore the 'Other' of heterosexual culture in many of their stories. Further, Gordon Legge and Jeff Noon point out that their readings and book audiences have as many females as males. But undoubtedly the glossy 90s male monthlies, *Arena*, *GQ*, *FHM*, *Maxim* as well as *Loaded*, have helped to market the repetitive beat generation fiction to an eager, young, male, consumer audience.

In America, in particular, this popular cultural change has been linked to the emergence of 'Generation X.' The first use of the moniker Generation X was in Charles Hamblett and Jane Deverson's pulp theory book in Britain in 1964. Then Billy Idol's mid-70s punk band adopted it. But in the 90s Douglas Coupland's books *Generation X*, *Shampoo Planet*, *Life after God*, *Microserfs*, *Polaroids from the Dead* and *Girlfriend in a Coma* and Richard Linklater's films *Slacker* and *Dazed and Confused*, alongside pop movies such as Ben Stiller's

*Reality Bites*, were widely touted in the international mass media as supposedly symbolising the emergence of a 'nineties generation' – that is those born in the 60s or 70s and labelled as (another) 'lost generation', 'twentysomethings', 'busters', 'doomers', 'slackers' or, simply, Generation X. These were said by fashionable media and cultural commentators to be the youth cultures which came after the 80s 'boomers', 'yuppies' and 'thirtysomethings'. For others they are the 'jilted generation', as British dance act The Prodigy's second LP proclaimed them, or alternatively the 'chemical generation', or what American 'alienated' youth chronicler Donna Gaines calls the 'fucked generation'.

Predictably, the cultural artefacts of this new formation (such as the British fanzine *The Idler*, or Richard Linklater's films) have been centred on 'white heterosexual masculinity' though alternative approaches – for instance Rose Troche's *Go Fish* film about young lesbian culture, Gregg Araki's *Totally F\*\*\*ed Up* about multiracial lesbian and gay teenagers in Los Angeles, and Rosa Liksom's Scandinavian short fictions *One Night Stands* – have all been presented in advertising, cultural criticism and media publicity as offshoots of the same Gen-X. There is an echo here of past confusions and mistaken media lumping together of fragments of youth cultures under one label, and the fact that Generation X was originally noted in the early 90s as a fundamentally North American trend is more illustrative of a general globalisation of culture throughout the world. For some writers, anyway, we are already past Generation X. As Arthur and Marilouise Kroker note in *Hacking the Future*: 'as we come under the pull of the year 2000, you can almost feel the shifting of the generations ... Slackers and those of the so-called Generation X were born postmodern but are still part of the chip generation oscillating between flesh and data. Now there's an entirely new generation: the digital generation. Post-chip, pure digital wonders of the 3rd millennium'.

The 80s blank generation fiction of Bret Easton Ellis, Jay McInerney and others has been anthologised and analysed. Disagreement about what to label such writing – downtown fiction or avant-pop for example – is less important than the fact that such culture is perceived as

, or literature based. As *The Face* magazine put it: ⌐n't think . . . that dance culture would be well suited to ⌐e. While dance music may be fluid and ephemeral there's few ⌐gs more solid than 200 pages of paperback. The clubland novel has a long, if chequered, history, from the cappuccino-fuelled Soho novels of Colin 'Absolute Beginners' MacInnes in the Fifties, to the coke-driven tales of decadent downtown youth in Manhattan and LA by Jay 'Bright Lights Big City' McInerney and Bret 'Less Than Zero' Easton Ellis in the Eighties . . . irrespective of the different forms of music they cover, each book raises the same doubt, because the novel form is peculiarly unsuited to tales of club culture. Films, TV and radio are all media that can express the transient nature of the nation's nightlife better than the . . . ethos of the novel (Not to say that cinema's attempt to capture the clubbing moment have been uniformly successful). Which perhaps proves the point that dance culture expresses itself best through itself: via the media of clubs and music . . . Perhaps the explosion of clubland novels should be no surprise; no more than the expression of the maturity of modern British club culture. Since the rebirth of British nightlife in the Eighties, underground dance music has crossed into the mainstream with increasing force . . . And a movement into the staid world of publishing is a logical progression'.

Cinematically these popular cultural shifts have certainly been problematic. *Trainspotting* is a very different film from the novel in feel and sense; in any case it deals with heroin use, not the more prevalent recreational drugs of LSD or Ecstasy which *The Acid House* movie takes on. Probably Justin Kerrigan's Cardiff based *Human Traffic* is the quintessential 90s drug culture film and plugs in to a young, cinema-going mass audience's experience of the weekend.

The dramatisation of some of the repetitive beat generation fiction has helped to redefine drama in the 90s and what critics conventionally think of as a theatre audience. When Irvine Welsh's *Trainspotting* was first put on as a play in London, he told me, the box office was so unused to dealing with cash paying customers – instead of pre-bookings by credit card – that the performance was delayed. I saw the later version at the Contact Theatre in Manchester and virtually every member of the audience was under 30. John King notes that the stage version of *The Football Factory* – dramatised by Paul Hodson who also wrote a one man version of *Fever Pitch* – opened to a packed audience more often found at the football ground than a theatre. When I caught the play, toured by Brighton Theatre Events, in Salford, half the audience wandered in and out of the energetic, in your face, ska-scored performance clutching beer cans provided by the theatre as if it was half time on a match day (before 80s laws like the Criminal Justice (Scotland) Act 1980 and the Sporting Events (Control of Alcohol etc.) Act 1985 introduced alcohol bans). That this changing sense of what theatre as popular culture might mean has led to controversy is not surprising. The British Council, for example, decided not to take *You'll Have Had Your Hole* to Belgium after its premiere run in Leeds because of some of the complaints about its language and subject matter.

## DIY, Fanzine Culture and the New Fiction Publishers

My own interest in telling the story in this book is twofold. Partly it is as a fan. Reading fiction by Gordon Legge, Pete Davies and Michael Bracewell in the late 80s I was starting to become aware of a different generation of writers who I enjoyed reading and wanted to find out more about them and their influences.

At this time I was also researching, and archiving, alternative media such as fanzines – popular music and football-based ones but also ecological and political-leaning 'zines – which if not exactly under-ground were certainly outside the mainstream. Small independent book publishing ventures, too, came into this arena. As I began researching the questions for the conversations which make up the bulk of this book I quickly discovered the importance of small scale DIY publishing – fanzines, booklets, books – to the story of the repetitive beat generation. The British literary 'zine in the 90s follows on from diverse US fanzines and literary magazines like *Between C and D* but it also steps, surprisingly perhaps, in the footsteps of the music and football fanzines of the 70s, 80s and 90s.

The roots of many of the authors are clearly in fanzine culture, especially football and music fanzines. *Rebel Inc* itself was essentially a literary fanzine, as were John King's *Two Sevens* and *Verbal* produced from London in the early 90s. *Clocktower Press* booklets put out by Duncan McLean in Edinburgh were in a similar do-it-yourself vein. From 1994 England also had Elaine Palmer's *Pulp Faction* collections and eventually Pulp Books.

In many ways the phenomenal success of *Trainspotting* was unexpected and unplanned. Scottish underground literary 'zine *Rebel Inc* welcomed the novel – unsurprisingly in view of *Rebel Inc*'s own role in Welshmania – as 'the best book ever written by man or woman . . . deserves to sell more copies than the Bible'. In 1993, the year of the publication of the novel, *Rebel Inc* published a quirky pamphlet by Welsh and its founder Kevin Williamson called *A Visitor's Guide to Edinburgh*.

It was the sort of low key thing that *Clocktower Press* had been doing for a number of months already. Frustrated by the time taken to get responses to his own efforts to publish stories, writer Duncan McLean created *Clocktower Press*, with fellow writer James Meek, in true entrepreneurial style. As he explains in *Ahead Of Its Time* – a *Clocktower Press* anthology which he edited – 'we'd do it ourselves. Taking inspiration from music and football fanzines we decided that glossy production and distribution in prestigious outlets was less important than getting our voices heard'.

In 1992 the fifth of the *Clocktower* booklets ('literary time bombs' as McLean has described them) was published. Entitled *Past Tense: Four Stories From a Novel* the booklet featured four Irvine Welsh stories which were later to be included in the novel *Trainspotting*. McLean, who had been running a writer's group in Muirhouse since 1991, takes up the story: 'Our slowest seller was undoubtedly *Past Tense: Four stories from a novel* by Irvine Welsh. Welsh had grown up in Muirhouse but was living in Leith by this time. His debut publication – "First Day of the Edinburgh Festival" – was in *New Writing Scotland 9* – edited by Janice Galloway and Hamish Whyte and published in October 1991. I liked that story a lot and asked Janice what she knew about its author: nothing. "Irvine Welsh is currently completing a brightly optimistic novel full of sympathetic, generously spirited characters", said his biographical note in *NWS*. Eventually I tracked him down, we met a few times, and in April 1992 *Clocktower Press* published *Past Tense*, with powerful illustrations by Peter Govan. In those days to write about heroin addicts on a run-down Edinburgh estate was far from the easy commercialism cynical critics often accuse Irvine of having adopted. Quite the opposite: only a few folk shared my enthusiasm for what he was doing. Luckily, one of those few was Kevin Williamson. When the first issue of *Rebel Inc* came out on 1 May, it had another great piece by Irvine in it . . . Kevin's commitment to the new writing that was starting to break out all over the east coast, combined with his talent for promotion, publicity and distribution, meant that *Rebel Inc* had an enormous impact; people all over the country, and in all the media, were talking about a literary magazine – a rare occurrence!'

## Conversations with the Repetitive Beat Generation

This book's main purpose is to tell the real story of how this new fiction emerged and how it was influenced by – and in turn influenced – the fast changing club and popular culture of the late twentieth century. Taking a selection of the novels, short stories, plays and films which make up the archive of the repetitive beat generation so far, the story is told through original interviews with some of the creative writers who talk about the sharpest counter cultural literary movement to emerge since the beat generation.

Yet the repetitive beat generation writers have a certain un-sympathetic, even antagonistic, relationship to the beat generation of Jack Kerouac, Allen Ginsberg and William Burroughs. For John King 'the actual Beat writers were good because they were trying to do something different but having said that they were all bankrolled by their mums and dads . . . The ideas were good but the actual content . . . was quite superficial'. Irvine Welsh 'wanted to like Burroughs and Kerouac more than I did . . . because of the influence that they had'. Gordon Legge has never quite finished *On The Road* however hard he has tried, though he enjoyed the later William Burroughs 'potboilers'. In many ways the authors of the repetitive beat generation were influenced more by punk than 'beat'. They are very definitely 'post-punk' in the historical sense even if they are soulboys and disco fans at heart like Irvine Welsh, the oldest of the bunch just into his forties. The repetitive beat generation writers in general barely take any direct inspiration from the writings of Jack Kerouac, Allen Ginsberg and William Burroughs or for that matter Gregory Corso, Lawrence Ferlinghetti, Michael McClure and Gary Snyder. Scotland-born writer Martin Millar told the *Guardian* that he realised that his knowledge 'of contemporary literature was poor and I thought I should fill in some of the gaps, so I bought a copy of *Naked Lunch* by William Burroughs, [which] had a profound effect on me. I hated it . . . I disliked it so intensely that I was obliged to throw it in the bin after a few chapters. Furthermore, I resolved to give up on modern fiction altogether'. The *Independent* quotes Alan Warner as being 'very suspicious of that Jack Kerouac thing. You know: "I've driven across America and now I'm going to write about it, explaining all my thoughts". Now all you need to write a book is an Oxbridge education and a coke habit. It all seems a bit self-indulgent to me; and because I'm a very insecure, private person, I'm cautious about using myself as material'.

In reality the 40s, 50s and 60s beat generation fiction and poetry was as much to do with incorporating other cultural forms into writing (Kerouac's free-form jazz writing) and the wide cultural influence of the writing on lifestyle (drugs, hitch-hiking, music) as its status as a post-war literary movement. The dance, rock and pop culture which provides the context for cultural production in novels, plays, poetry and film in the 90s is massively influential on the repetitive beat generation. New fiction in the 90s refers in many ways to the beats and the 40s and 50s in the way that it immerses itself in an 'alternative' culture of the times.

The authors interviewed in the following pages are inevitably a selection or sample of the repetitive beat generation. In many ways they are a diverse group themselves, coming from different cities, countries, areas and cultures in Britain and Ireland. However they are distinct from at least two other groups of related fiction writers. The 'American Blank Generation' which Elizabeth Young and Graham Caveney wrote about are really more related to the 'yuppie' (young urban professional) era of the 80s. Meanwhile, miscellaneous authors from Britain have also set their novels or short stories in the world of youth cults, media, drugs and popular culture with varying degrees of success: Martin Amis, Hanif Kureishi, Nick Hornby, John Williams, Geoff Dyer and Michael Bracewell have all fictionalised bohemian lifestyles in the era of the breakdown of the consensus of post-war Britain.

However, these authors are united more by what DJ Taylor calls 'the literary consequences of Mrs Thatcher' in their 'Thatcher novels'. The 'repetitive beat generation' on the other hand begin to map out, in very different and often contradictory ways, the new counter cultures which have grown up in the wake of yuppiedom and so-called Thatcher-ism, the free market, economic globalisation and the New Right. As Irvine Welsh argues, house music and its dance derivatives emerging in the late 80s were the inspiration for a whole swathe of fiction: from pop journalist Paolo Hewitt's club and party novel published by Jeff Barrett's Heavenly record company to Welsh's own 'creative' use of house rhythms in his stunning dialect prose. *Trainspotting* – like *The Acid House* and *Marabou Stork Nightmares* – is the product of more than just a 'literary' mind; it is steeped in a millennial culture where old barriers (black/white, gay/straight etc.) are breaking down.

The repetitive beat generation authors interviewed in this book wrote a cultural history as it was happening, but they wrote it in fiction, not in the language of sociology, history, jurisprudence or politics. They used all kinds of forms of story-telling – science fiction, horror, crime fiction, drug fiction, short story, reportage, biography, performance art – to tell the fascinating tale of the last counter cultures – and much much, more – of the twentieth century. Although poetry has once again been touted as the new rock and roll with the corporate hype surrounding multi-media artists such as Murray Lachlan Young, new fiction has been the only real contender in the 90s, despite many of the authors' interest in non-prose forms. All of the fourteen writers featured in the conversations in this book, many of whom have to some extent followed in the wake of Irvine Welsh in the 90s, tell their criss-crossing stories, individual and collective, of how they got here and where they are going, in their own very different styles, languages and accents. This is the repetitive beat generation *live*: no overdubs, no remixes.

# Conversations

*Nicholas Blincoe*

# New Crime Wave
Nicholas Blincoe

*Born in the mid-1960s Nicholas Blincoe is from Rochdale near Manchester. He is author of* Acid Casuals, Jello Salad, Manchester Slingback, The Dope Priest, *a collection of short stories* My Mother Was a Bankrobber *and other stories and co-editor of an anthology* All Hail The New Puritans.

*Crime fiction is the genre Blincoe chooses for the oblique showcasing of Manchester's pop cultural history that three of his novels perform.* Acid Casuals, Jello Salad *and* Manchester Slingback, *as well as the short story 'Ardwick Green' in* Disco Biscuits, *and 'English Astronaut' in* Disco 2000, *represent an application of American crime fiction style to the concerns of 1980s and 1990s contemporary youth culture and pop history. In* The Dope Priest *he reinvents the political thriller. Nicholas Blincoe argues that he is part of a new wave of crime fiction but also accepts the overdone label of the 'chemical generation'. His first novel* Acid Casuals *was written fast in the early 1990s as the culture was developing. In Blincoe's novels rave and acid house and Manchester's post-punk and gay pop scenes feature strongly. As Michael Bracewell, himself one of Britain's outstanding novelists and cultural commentators and now a Manchester resident, put it, 'Blincoe makes a valuable literary addition to Manchester's peerless ability to define itself through its popular culture'.*

*A former Factory recording artist with Meatmouth, Blincoe went to Warwick University in the 1980s where he developed his interest in pulp/cult fiction.* Manchester Slingback *won the Macallan Crime Writers' Association Silver Dagger Award for fiction in 1998 and in 1999 he became an editor at Hodder Headline. He lives in London and writes crime fiction reviews for the* Observer.

*I caught up with him on his trips back to Manchester and we talked after he had given a talk to students and police on 'drug novels'.*

**STEVE REDHEAD** What place do you think you have in the range of 90s new fiction authors like Irvine Welsh, Jeff Noon, Alan Warner and others?

**NICHOLAS BLINCOE** I have been much more comfortable about labels than other people – maybe that's coming from philosophy, with taxonomies all the time. But I don't think it's that actually. I think it's just coming from a culture where I was a punk one week and I was a mod the next week and then I was a punk again. I feel it's a bit churlish to start saying 'no don't label me'. I tend to have two labels. I didn't choose either of them but I'm not particularly aghast at either of them. One is the chemical generation, the other is the new wave of crime fiction. I can see both of them.

**S. R.** Were you aware of these authors when you started writing fiction?

**N. B.** I didn't know about Irvine Welsh unfortunately when I wrote *Acid Casuals*. I'm really quite embarrassed by it but there wasn't any way of knowing. As I was finishing *Acid Casuals* I noticed there was this book out, *The Acid House*. So I went out of my way to read some reviews of it. Although I was intrigued, I wasn't very intrigued. I thought well I'll put that one on the back burner. It sounded to me – and I don't want to quote people, I just can't remember – as though they were saying he was in the style of Samuel Beckett. I'd always liked Samuel Beckett. They actually did say Samuel Beckett 'cos there was that idea of the monologue, and he is a monologuist. So it gave me no idea at all of what the book was about. And that was *The Acid House*, it wasn't *Trainspotting*. I never, ever read a review of *Trainspotting*.

**S. R.** Why did you want to write fiction? How did you get into it?

**N. B.** I wanted to be a writer for a long while but then didn't. I wrote some stuff as a teenager and it was pretty poor. There were things that really made me want to write when I came to writing again. One was the new crime fiction coming out of America – like Elmore Leonard, James Ellroy and Charles Willeford, Chester Himes and Jim Thompson and Carl Hiaasen. Writers who were very funny, very dark but also pulp fiction so it was that idea, that kind of liberation that you can be a pulp writer. My younger brother turned me on to all that kind of stuff – he's only vaguely younger, he's only a year and a half younger – he was the person who introduced me to crime fiction and that was a kind of real liberation. I'd been reading the 'canon' previous to that. Or I'd been reading Beat Generation literature. Or I'd been reading sixties and seventies American literature. But I wasn't reading that much eighties British literature. Martin Amis I loved, by the time I actually got down to writing. I read *Money* first and I read that virtually at the time it came out 'cos I was at art college then and I got to know the lecturer who lent me the book. So I actually read that in 1981 or 1982, whatever time it came out in hardback and that really blew me away. And actually one of my teenage novels is virtually a pastiche of *Money*. I've got several teenage novels: one is a pastiche of William Burroughs and one is a pastiche of Martin Amis. I like all the books before it apart from the one written – I can't remember the name of it – from the point of view of the woman which stands out as being odd. I like *Success*, *The Rachel Papers*, *Dead Babies*. I was very disappointed with his eighties work. Maybe he's a seventies writer or something. There aren't that many writers from the eighties I like at all. Some annoy me tremendously and it's not very cool to say it but I never liked Salman Rushdie. It's become problematic because of the issue – as a novelist I don't like him – but the issue is 'we can write anything we want and fundamentalists of any kind shouldn't tell us what to do.'

**S. R.** What influences did you have? What were you were trying to do?

**N. B.** I went to University [Warwick] late when I was twenty after two years at art college. I had written the teenage novels before then. I went to do Philosophy and Literature. The idea was that I wanted to write more intelligent types of novels than the ones I'd written and a lot more intelligent than the ones I was reading because although I really liked *On The Road* – and I read all the Beat things – I really didn't like Kerouac's other stuff, and I didn't want to be known as a stupid writer or whatever. So I was trying to do something. *On The Road* was definitely an influence on my teenage novels – that energy. I know all about Kerouac. I probably know more about his life than I do about his literature 'cos I've read the big Kerouac biography. And I'm a huge fan of Burroughs. One of the big things in my life was seeing Burroughs read in 1982 at the Hacienda. That was a huge thing. They would both be influences – Burroughs more than Kerouac. Kerouac I've always seen as being a bit like DH Lawrence. That kind of free spirit thing isn't really me. I'm much more of an uptight, neurotic type of character. I identified much more with Burroughs but kind of reacting against himself 'cos he'll talk about transcendental experiences but that's not what his books are like: his books are like pulp fiction. From *Junky* onwards it's clear that he's got that kind of offbeat, noir voice in his work.

**S. R.** Can you say something about your interest in Philosophy and Literature? How did that connect to crime fiction?

**N. B.** I went to do a degree in Philosophy and Literature and liked Philosophy so much that I stayed on to do more and then did a PhD. My PhD is on Jacques Derrida, but it is on the way he uses the term 'economics' as a kind of metaphor to describe styles of writing. But I took him totally literally and said 'what is philosophy?' and taking a few major philosophers asked what has been their reaction to economics. It's very discursive for a PhD and I think I was lucky that I passed first time. In retrospect I think I was very lucky I passed. By this time I was living in Manchester, commuting to Warwick. It was the 'acid house' time and I was doing quite a lot of acid. In lots of ways I'm surprised I passed. But Warwick was a good place. My supervisor was Dr Nick Land – roughly around that time he was the boyfriend of another academic, Sadie Plant – and we didn't really see eye to eye on everything but we enjoyed each other's company. I was reading both Derrida and crime fiction. I hated Derrida by this time. I liked Deleuze much more. This was Nick Land's influence. I had been reading crime fiction all the time, I read a huge amount. There was a big caucus of us who were fans of James Ellroy. The PhD is experimental as far as PhDs go but the way in which it does react to my real life is the title: 'Deconstruction and Depression'. It's about how philosophers dealt with economics but also what they meant by depression and that's been really the experience of the eighties. In the early 1980s I was unemployed and then when I finished my first degree there was another depression so people were finding it difficult to get jobs. There was a boom in between, there was a boom when I was doing my MA and there was a depression when I was doing my PhD so that kind of rocky economic thing was important. Also at university I actually got called a Thatcher Youth all the time by all the Professors. It really fucked me off. They'd had such a cushy life and I really hated that. And the idea of finishing a PhD in two years after my MA – I was getting slagged off for doing it in the time limit that I was being paid to do it. I had to do it in the time, I just didn't have a choice. The idea of spending seven years over a PhD! I was critical of them and I got called a Thatcher Youth. I went to university in 1985 and I graduated with my PhD in 1992.

**S. R.** What about pop culture? How did that influence you?

**N. B.** It's a weird thing. I'm from Rochdale. I'd been in bands. I'd always been in bands from being about fifteen, playing at school and playing in garage punk bands and things. I left school when I was sixteen and I actually got – although I'd actually left school and was going to art college – thrown out of school after my band played and I slashed at my stomach with a Stanley knife. It was a kind of Iggy Pop thing. So I'd played in bands. I've got very little musical talent but I've got this real enthusiasm for punk. In 1986 when I was already at University some of my friends who were much better at music were all listening to this imported hip hop. I listened to a lot of stuff but the thing that really stood out for us being white and from Rochdale was the Beastie Boys. So we got well into the Beastie Boys. I got signed to Factory very quickly but we were only six months ahead of the curve. And in six months time everybody had heard of the Beastie Boys. That was 1986 and 1987. I went on tour with the Age of Chance in 1987. So that's when I was signed to Factory but I actually was then a student at Warwick. And the two other people in Meatmouth – my friend Mark Whitham was a student at a London art college, and the other person was Greg Keefe and he was in Big Flame. We got Greg Keefe in slightly later. There's only one record, it's called 'Meatmouth is Murder' so it's like a Smiths piss-take or pastiche. We weren't anti-The Smiths. We broke up because while touring I fell out with Greg Keefe really. It wasn't a great tour either. We toured with Age Of Chance and they were just past their peak. Also I think we just ran out of time. But I quite like the single. The Rochdale connection is that the person who produced our demo tapes is Lisa Stansfield's boyfriend.

**S. R.** Was it crime fiction then or pop culture which gave you your style?

**N. B.** I think the style comes equally from both. Writing rap, writing hip hop stuff and listening to hip hop all the time – I still listen to hip hop. Even when I was going to raves all the time I really only listened to hip hop. That use of language – and there are certain figures that stand head and shoulders above the rest – and listening to the way they use language, it enters English so quickly, especially I think in Manchester. You read reviews, you read interviews with people, you can hear people in the street, you can even point to it in something like *NME*, you point to a Manchester musician and they speak in something that on the page is like some weird hybrid Caribbean-American-Manchester and if you hear it then it sounds like something weird in a strong Manchester accent. I used to really listen to the way that people talked all the time 'cos I'm not actually from Manchester, I'm from Rochdale, which is a small town so it's obviously slightly out of the loop. So the way people talked in Manchester has always been fascinating to me from being fifteen when I heard Perries (Perry boys, Manchester's casuals) going 'I'll see yoh' and 'seeyoh mate' and 'hiyoh'. I'm a huge fan of Mark E. Smith and the way that he uses language. There are a lot of Fall references in all my books. I'm trying to signal that this is the type of writing that's influencing me, and Elmore Leonard obviously I think, that kind of third person narration that switches from character to character. Elmore Leonard's virtually got a copyright on that and that's influenced a lot of people besides me; like Martin Amis in his latest novel, and Quentin Tarantino, and he's said it all the time as well. I'm too young to have been a punk but punk was one of the big things and people say about the DIY ethic and all that but the big thing for me was that you like contemporary stuff and you champion contemporary stuff over the 'canon'. That's the big thing for me but I didn't really do it in fiction. One of my teenage novels – they're really awful! – is a pastiche of James Joyce. I never got out from the shadow of literature. And I think one of the reasons maybe deconstruction was exciting to me was 'how do you deal with this overwhelming weight of this canon?' And people say that Kerouac was influenced by the jazz generation, and he was superficially, but you read interviews with him and he's actually claiming that he's a reincarnation of James Joyce and he's saying that he loves DH Lawrence. He had huge problems with the 'canon'. The whole pulp thing to me was suddenly realising that instead of this tradition there's a whole other tradition. And you can take it all the way back to Daniel Defoe. But you don't have to do that. You can just say Charles Willeford, Jim Thompson, Chester Himes, Iceberg Slim – there's a lot of people reading the same stuff. It was that excitement of 'the canon means nothing'. There's a whole new way of thinking about fiction, new exciting stuff coming out of America and also the big idea of being English which has never been a big thing for me 'cos coming from Manchester, Englishness has tended to be more of a London thing.

**S. R.** Do you think that new or cult fiction has in fact been the way a particular contemporary history has been written in the late 1980s and 1990s?

**N. B.** *Acid Casuals* was pretty soon after it. The book came out in 1995. When I really thought 'I want to write fiction again', when I had the energy to write fiction again, that novel was actually planned around 1990 and 1992 and I wrote it very fast because the plot was just there, so I did the first draft actually in six weeks, which was really hammering it. I *am* really writing it as it's happening. I realised just how dark things were getting, but reading the Matthew Collin book *Altered State* I realised it was actually much darker in reality than I had made it in my novel. The book was finished in 1994, I started the first draft around Christmas 1993 and finished the draft in February 1994. *Manchester Slingback* is the first 'history' of that period of gay culture in Manchester. I am not really much of a historian. I am weak on research. People keep describing me as a journalist, but I am not a very good journalist. I have been picking up opinion pieces but I just don't do my research. I couldn't do it any other way. I want to write what the immediate, contemporary history is but through fiction. One of the big stories of the 1980s and 1990s is the moving overground of gay culture, and Manchester is maybe one of the best places in the world to write about it. There's also the way it was policed in the eighties and the way young offenders are treated. Crime fiction – like the rest of society – has recently made paedophiles into the great demons of society. This was noticeable in American crime fiction, even stuff that I liked did this; James Ellroy does it. They are the absolute evil, the touchstones. Part of the reason I tackled abuse in *Manchester Slingback* wasn't simply because it was happening, because I wasn't aware of that at the time. The reason I was drawn to crime fiction was contemporary history. If you're doing contemporary history, it's got to be good contemporary history. Some of the stuff, some of the American stuff! I really don't like Andrew Vachss at all, I think his moralising is just bollocks. If you're going to do contemporary history – which is what I want to do – you've got to do it in a dramatic, entertaining form that's not afraid to be funny and not afraid to be sentimental and not afraid to be hard and it's got to be good.

*Sarah Champion*

# Generation E
Sarah Champion

Sarah Champion was born in the early 1970s and comes from Manchester. She is editor of four anthologies of 'new fiction'. Disco Biscuits, Disco 2000, Shenanigans and Fortune Hotel have all been commercially successful. Sarah Champion proudly touts the whole enterprise as chock full of younger writers, the twentysomethings like herself and the rest in their thirties.

As editor of volumes of stories deeply set in Generation E culture over the decade of acid house and rave since 1987, Champion is well placed to help put the genesis into perspective. Editor of the fanzine Scam and author of And God Created Manchester, an heretical history of the Manchester music scene at the end of the 1980s when she was one of the sharpest – and youngest – pop journalists in Britain, Sarah Champion went on to work at Volume where numerous jungle, electro, techno and house CD collections were produced.

Disco Biscuits (club slang for Ecstasy), an anthology of nineteen stories, collects together what the publishers called 'new fiction from the chemical generation', or tales from the accelerated culture of Generation E. Disco 2000 is a follow up collection, another anthology of nineteen short stories which take place in the last hours of December 31, 1999. The commercial success of the anthologies encouraged other publishers to anthologise 'end of the century' stories and the original publisher Hodder Headline soon commissioned a third volume from Champion along with Dublin DJ and video producer Donal Scannell, this time collecting together cutting edge Irish fiction. The fourth was a similar concept applied to travel writing published by Penguin.

Sarah Champion now lives in London. I talked with her in a café bar in an Arts Centre in Manchester on a rare trip back home.

**STEVE REDHEAD** Why did you choose fiction – as you say in *Disco Biscuits* – as a version of contemporary history?

**SARAH CHAMPION** Originally I was approached by Simon Prosser at Sceptre [Hodder Headline] possibly to write a history of 'Acid House' because I'd been working as a journalist in Manchester and I'd been writing about house and electronic music. Apart from being really overwhelmed by the idea – because at that point there weren't any books – and not knowing where to begin I didn't really feel it would capture the experience that I'd been through and that a lot of people had been through. Once you start writing a history like that, you have to decide on specific definitive dates, specific records, specific DJs, specific books whereas the way 'house' was spread across England it was much more a personal experience for everyone who came into contact with it. The idea, the way that it came about, was that it wasn't about the DJ or celebrity, it was the antithesis of the 'rock star' – it was much more about the people on the dance floor – they were the stars. So once you start writing a history you lose contact with that.

And also just around that time I'd bought this expensive sort of coffee table book which had hundreds of interviews with people who went to Woodstock. And I was reading it and one thing it made me think was 'well the things I've seen in the last few years in Manchester and beyond are as exciting as that time in a different way – why isn't it documented?' And also just reading people's words sort of took you back there. So I considered interviewing hundreds of people around the country about 'Acid House' and British clubculture. From there also came the idea that if people are going to tell a story maybe fiction would be the ideal format. At about the same time as this I was going in bookshops looking for something to read, looking for something contemporary. The most contemporary 'cool' books were things like *High Fidelity* by Nick Hornby which is a fortysomething boys' nostalgia book about the early 1970s. There was nothing contemporary at all so the idea came together to combine those things. It was more about finding writers that I wanted to read. It was just a hobby project really. I saw *The Acid House* by Irvine Welsh in the shops. I bought it when it came out. Basically I bought it, took it home, read the first two pages and went 'uh?!'. I put it aside for a really long time because – and maybe that was subconsciously why I started the whole thing – I'd bought it thinking it was a book about 'Acid House', or about contemporary times. Heroin for me was just like a completely different generation – I couldn't relate to any of it initially. So I just put it aside completely. Then with Irvine Welsh's success it was the words I could relate to. Even ravers who have never had heroin – or drugs other than recreational drugs – relate to Irvine Welsh more than any other books in the shops. And at the same time I was a really big fan of Jeff Noon. I'd come across Alan Warner's *Morvern Callar* which referred – if only in passing – to Ibiza. I just wanted to extend that really and find more writers. It was just purely word of mouth. I just asked around. Initially it was mentioned on KISS FM that we wanted to do stories about clubbing – I don't think that anything that came of that actually got printed. We had about eighty stories from KISS FM where people were writing down their experiences, all kind of semi-fictional: they were obviously people's real experiences. But there was not anything good enough to be printed as a story. The story that sums up every single one that was sent in to KISS FM was Mike Benson's in *Disco Biscuits*, just a complete stream of consciousness, no-punctuation version of a typical night out, off your face. In a way, that captured everything in the eighty stories. Mike Benson was writing sleevenotes for Howie B. Since then he's done lots of little booklets of almost poetry. I guess people, when they're trying to write novels, they write short stories but I don't think they had been a particularly saleable thing. When I came up with the idea I was told by Sceptre, by various people, that volumes of short stories only sell 3,000 copies. But also a lot of people's first novels only sell 3,000 copies. With Irvine Welsh in it they thought it would sell at least 7,000. So it was all a nice surprise that we could change the market.

**S. R.** Do you think you were keying into something with collections of fiction at that time?

**S. C.** Basically, for ten years before that, since I was fourteen, I was doing music journalism. I moved to London in about 1991 and that was when I started purely dance journalism. I worked for *Mixmag* and *Melody Maker* writing about techno, ambient, electronica, clubculture.

In a way there was not a lot to say and I felt that all of those magazines equally missed the point. At the time of 'Acid House' I think there were only a couple of writers who got it. One was Jack Barron at *NME*. There should have been some kind of 'Gonzo' journalism to capture the spirit but there wasn't. *NME* wasn't very good. It had Paolo Hewitt writing on the music industry and it had Jack Barron writing. Apart from that there was really nothing. And then when the dance pages emerged in most papers and the dance magazines emerged they were very much doing features on DJs, counting the BPMs [beats per minute], dividing it into genres. There didn't seem to be any room for writing. If you look back to rock writing it had an energy – there were characters. All that seemed to be missing. So that was part of the idea as well. Somehow there was this thing that had happened that had changed a lot of people's lives but hadn't been written about at all and it just didn't seem to work in journalism. Journalism didn't seem to capture it.

**S. R.** Is that when you started doing work with Volume – where you had CDs and booklets about the music like the excellent two-volume drum 'n' bass *Breakbeat Science* and also the *Trance Europe Express* stuff – because you got fed up with mainstream music journalism?

**S. C.** Obviously I didn't start the *Trance Europe Express* series – Helen Mead started that (actually she has a short story in *Disco 2000*) and again was a journalist with Jack Barron at *NME*. She started the *Trance Europe Express* series which was CDs of electronic music and articles about all the artists. That was really great and that was something that went all over the world. Basically because people could buy the music and it was so anonymous and this way they could hear the track and read about the artist. Now that's finished I'm putting together a thing called *Southside Stories* which is a CD based in Brixton where I lived for about four years. It's not really financially viable to do a big expensive colour book and a CD but that's ultimately the idea. Multimedia – music and books. With Sceptre I just went off and did it. The whole thing with *Disco Biscuits* was pure accident. I knew absolutely nothing about publishing whatsoever. But I think that was a big advantage. Because I just broke all the rules by not knowing that there were any. I decided what I wanted on the cover and told them all the 'underground' dance magazines to send copies to, to get reviewed in, automatically assuming that the launch party wouldn't be glasses of wine, that it would be a big event with readings from the book. I automatically thought there should be a soundtrack CD. It is, I think, the only one – apart from *Disco 2000* – that's ever been done; certainly the only one that's been done for an anthology. Also I just automatically assumed there should be flyers. Being involved with record labels I thought 'CD' because that's what I know and it worked – it actually reached people who probably wouldn't have just walked into a bookshop.

**S. R.** What were the readings – and other promotional events – for *Disco Biscuits* like?

**S. C.** Nicholas Blincoe and myself did one in Paris – that was OK. But the best one was the one with Arthrob. It was partly like an Irvine Welsh fan club night – he was the biggest person on there. But there were videos, visuals, and DJs and readings. It was very chaotic. You couldn't get anywhere near the front. When Irvine Welsh 'played' that room was actually crammed and the dance floor was next door, next door we had Marshall Jefferson and LTJ Bukem – the dance floor was excellent – but everyone wanted to hear Irvine Welsh. It wouldn't have had the same atmosphere in a bookshop, there's no way. But also Jeff Noon did a reading, Nicholas Blincoe read, and I think they were kind of freaked out because they are more used to reading in bookshops. I'm not sure I'm going to continue the idea of readings in clubs. Writers get a bit freaked out when people talk and don't listen. But it's a lot more challenging because at a reading in a bookshop everyone's going to be really adoring and quiet. It hasn't really established itself. I suppose it is a little bit too weird and impractical. We did the same thing at Back To Basics in Leeds. We had one in Manchester at Paradise Factory. That was really good because Charlie Hall did a reading and then went and DJ-ed. That was one of the things that was really quite cool about *Disco Biscuits*, partly because I didn't deal with any agents whatsoever, just the writers themselves not the publishing establishment. Mike Benson's experience was writing sleevenotes, 'Q' was ten years ago producing chapters of his novel *Deadmeat* and flogging them outside Woolworths and finally after years and years he's got a novel, a website and does performances where he performs the book with a soundtrack. Charlie Hall is obviously a DJ and his was the most popular story. I suppose because it was true!

**S. R.** What about *Disco 2000*? Was that contracted at the same time as *Disco Biscuits*?

**S. C.** *Disco Biscuits* was just a one-off. The advance was £5,000 split between everybody. It was only supposed to sell 7,000 copies. It sold 60,000! But it sold almost all of those in the first six months in 1997. I didn't realise the significance of that even for myself. I think it really did freak everyone out, 'what's this, it's weird'. And I don't know who said it now but someone had said 'surely people who go clubbing don't read'. I can't remember now where it came from but there was that general assumption and I think it's partly to do with the fact that electronic music doesn't have words and therefore it can't be 'intelligent'. It did prove that people do read and they want books that they can relate to. Sceptre came back to me and said we want another *Disco Biscuits*, do another book of stories about clubbing and I said 'no I've done that'. *Disco 2000* is something completely different and I think it's loads better because the subject matter is completely fascinating. It's just one of those subjects that absolutely fascinates people of my age. For years and years everyone's been thinking of that date [December 31, 1999] and talked about what they would do, and it's getting closer. *Disco 2000* sold about 35,000 copies. The same thing happened with the authors – I just went to all my favourite 'cult' writers. *Disco Biscuits* was anyone I could find I thought could write about what was happening in Britain around 'Acid House' or everything after, and *Disco 2000* was just me going to all my favourite writers. I didn't get William Gibson but I got Neal Stephenson. I think *Disco 2000* is the best one. I don't think it got recognised in any of the reviews because no one really read it, they just decided they were going to have a 'chemical' fiction backlash which was a bit frustrating because the whole idea was that it wasn't the same at all.

**S. R.** What about the Irish 'after dark' fiction anthology with Donal Scannell? Did Sceptre come to you after the best-selling success story of the first two anthologies?

**S. C.** I don't think *Shenanigans* is going to be a best seller in the same way. It was purely from Michael McLoughlin, who is a PR person for English publishers in Ireland. He is a publicist. He publicises all the really cool stuff, English and Irish, in Ireland. I think it was his idea. He was just fed up with the Irish literary scene and how it was even more pretentious and boring than the English one. He thought that something like this was needed in Ireland. Donal Scannell had spoken to me when I was about fourteen – it's all a bit hazy but I do remember speaking to him.

He's a hot shot in Dublin. It's just a question of the same attitude, people slightly outside the literary scene. The only author I knew when I started to collect the stories for *Shenanigans* was Mike McCormack. His *Getting It in the Head* – along with Alex Garland's *The Beach* – are the best two books I'd read in the last few years. 'Getting It In The Head' was something totally different, not like anything else, more like an American writer than an Irish writer. All three of the anthologies have been about changing people's attitudes and were from a fan's point of view, rather than a literary point of view, good writing, what people want to read about.

**S. R.** Were you conscious that *Disco Biscuits* was basically male writers?

**S. C.** It *was* all men! It was really frustrating. There were women writers – a quarter of the authors – originally commissioned for *Disco Biscuits* but it was just one of those things, for whatever reason each of them were unable to do their story. Laura Hird I hadn't heard of then. I still think there's no female Irvine Welsh for instance. I don't know whether it's just my taste but most of the writers I have always liked have been male, but they've also been American. My favourite novels, all the underground fiction and cult fiction that I've generally been into, have been American. I'm not really sure why. William Gibson, Neal Stephenson. When I was about fourteen I started reading things like Jack Kerouac and Charles Bukowski. Ultimately there doesn't seem to be that many female versions, female equivalents. I was quite surprised though when I read that anthology of women's 'beat' writing and I was really amazed that I hadn't heard of any of these people before. So I think they were there; they just never got published. In our case with the Irish one I had to make a conscious effort to make sure there were enough men in it! Because for some reason in Ireland it's different – there are a lot of cool writers who are women.

**S. R.** What about your own writing? You've done lots of different non-fiction – you're editing a travel book – have you ever written fiction?

**S. C.** I tried to. I tried to write a novel about 'Madchester' when I was here but it was terrible. So I threw it away. Now I've read Nicholas Blincoe's *Acid Casuals* and *Manchester Slingback* he's said almost everything that needs to be said. Nicholas Blincoe was another person who I was aware of when I was looking for writers. He should be a star in Manchester.

I keep having a go at fiction but I've not really got the confidence. I think there are a lot of things that haven't been written about which is how I came to this in the first place. A similar thing happened with the travel book I'm editing called *Fortune Hotel* for Penguin. I would go to the travel writers section of a bookshop and it was the most boring section of the bookshop and again not really related to most people's experiences. So the new book is an anthology of travel writing. All the anthologies I've done are completely different from the way I planned. I don't know what I thought this one was going to be – more of a backpackers' novel – but I've actually ended up with a sort of strange dark-side-of-hotel-rooms anthology. They are a mixture of fiction and non-fiction, you can't really tell. The ones that are fiction are based on the writers' real experiences. Alex Garland may be in it. I was trying to get different people. Nicholas Blincoe, Will Self, Dennis Cooper, hopefully Irvine Welsh, Toby Litt, Emer Martin, there's a crossover with the others but I was trying to find new people. It does seem to be difficult to find people who are not of the literary mainstream, who haven't gone to Oxford or Cambridge. After *Disco 2000* I'd still not been to a publishing party. In the summer I accidentally went to some publishing parties and I was actually really shocked by the way everyone was. A different planet! Really posh, not just middle-class but upper middle-class! I found them really difficult to understand. I can see why all the novels that get published are by people who have been to Oxford or Cambridge or one of those creative writing courses. I thought there would be lots of people like Simon Prosser [editor at Sceptre and now at Penguin] but there aren't – I keep meeting editors now and they'd sign up foreign novels that they've never read, any novel which is written by someone who gets a good grade at the creative writing courses, or by anyone who is a friend of theirs from university – very competently written but basically absolutely boring. Simon Prosser I really rate for taking a chance on this. I think he was quite prepared to take the stick. The stick that we got when *Disco 2000* came out was unbelievable, even from people who are intelligent enough to know better. The worst one was when I did this interview for BBC Radio 4 – they basically said 'are all these writers going to be around in 5 years time?' It really stumped me and I wasn't articulate enough to answer on the day, and I tried to answer it politely and in fact what I should have said was that it was absurd because they're talking about Douglas Coupland and Neal Stephenson. It was just the most absurd and insulting question.

The thing that's most insulting about the whole thing is that tens and tens and tens and tens of these dinner party novels, thirtysomething *High Fidelity* novels, come out written by posh university graduates – and every now and again one of them is good and that's fine. But you're not allowed to write a bad 'working-class' book. They might hype it up for a little while for a novelty but they really don't want it. Because of *Trainspotting* and *Disco Biscuits* and whatever a lot of bad books came out in that genre but so what? I really want to read more books that I can relate to.

**S. R.** What has been the reaction in other countries to the anthologies? Do they have independent or maverick publishers too?

**S. C.** Europe has done really well. I think that's because dance culture is a pan-European thing. The same music is popular in all the countries, people can understand it. *Disco Biscuits* they're publishing this year in Italian, French and Greek. The French one is especially good because we had a launch party and people like *Liberation* took it seriously as a social document which is in a way partly something I wanted to do, but I don't know whether people in Britain take it that seriously. If you look at *Disco Biscuits* it's not a celebration of 'Acid House' – it's quite bleak. All the writers are from different backgrounds but they do sum up these times over the last ten years. Stories about being on the dole, whatever. In France they understood that, the whole thing. The thing about Britain is that it is so small. Everybody knows what's going on quite quickly. Whereas in America rave culture is quite a big underground thing – amongst the white kids – but the people in the publishing industry are so far removed that they literally have no idea that any underground culture even exists. The general response from America about *Disco Biscuits* is that it is too British. It's just different over there. Drugs are seen in such a different way over there. They haven't had such a strong recreational drug thing. But they'll sign up *Shenanigans* because it's Irish!

Emer Martin's book *Breakfast In Babylon* is a novel that somehow shouldn't be written in terms of the publishing industry because it's about a weird underground scene of people who travel around Europe, and in fact the book – by Wolfhound, an independent Dublin press – is difficult to find. I do think independent publishers like Pulp Faction/Books are brilliant. Steve Aylett's story was in *Techno Pagan* one of Pulp Faction's issues, it was just such a good story I wanted to reprint it in *Disco 2000*. Again *Pulp Faction*/Books is unique. Elaine Palmer runs that. And what *Rebel Inc* do is unique. They publish books which I don't think would ever get published elsewhere because they're too quirky. In America it does seem that there's a lot more chance for independent publishers. Ringpull Press – before they went bust – in Manchester were brilliant; they would have brought out half these books. I got interested in them because I like Jeff Noon's books – I did a bit of work, publicity, on those books *Vurt* and *Pollen*.

**S. R.** What did people actually say or write to you about the books? Was there anything that surprised you about the response apart from the sales success?

**S. C.** When *Disco Biscuits* came out I was quite nervous – I thought people would think it was rubbish and that was my biggest fear, that it would get laughed at. But it got the best reviews in magazines like *Mixmag*. One of the papers said it wasn't realistic but everyone else thought it was the closest book to their experiences. It's not perfect and it's not a literary masterpiece – it's kind of ropey in places – but people liked it. The best comment was when we went to Back To Basics in Leeds a guy came up – I think he was one of the roadies – and he said 'I've not read any books since I've left school and I've just read *Disco Biscuits* and it's brilliant!'

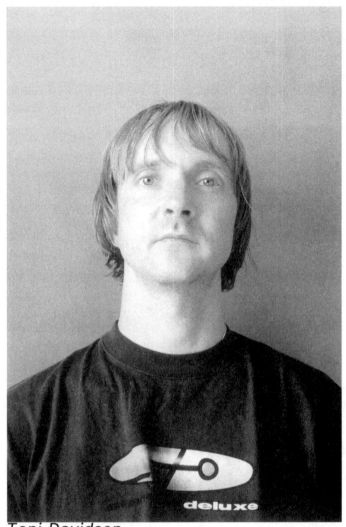

Toni Davidson

# **Scar Culture**
Toni Davidson

*Born in Ayr in the mid-1960s Toni Davidson is author of* Scar Culture, *an acclaimed first novel which has seen him marked out as a major new fiction talent.*

*In 1989 he was editor of* And Thus Will I Freely Sing *which was Scotland's first collection of gay and lesbian writing, published by Polygon shortly after the Tories had passed section 28 of the Local Government Act 1988. He saw it as championing writing by people who lived 'north of the south-east of England'. He is editor of a collection of stories called* Intoxication: An Anthology of Stimulant-Based Writing *published by Serpent's Tail in 1998. He points out in his introduction to the anthology that there has been a real upsurge in 'stimulant-based' writing: 'The canvas is so much broader now in terms of both cultural influences – from clubs to music to film – and the increasing, almost mundane, unsensational aspect to recreational drug use'. Refuting the myth that such drug use is simply tied to a new, laddish tendency in the culture of the end of the century, Toni Davidson adds that 'we are discovering that women can be both acute observers and active participants in drug culture'. His short fiction writing has appeared in* Rebel Inc, Gay Scotland, A Queer Tribe *and* Queer Words.

*A forgotten general influence in the development of 'cult' or 'new' fiction is that of performance art. Toni Davidson was involved with groups like Flow and ISO in Scotland and he and other performers read at events organised by literary fanzines like* Rebel Inc *in the days when cult fiction was seen as less fashionable than it is now. The spoken word, as he says, was often mixed in with music and various other performance arts rather than story-telling being confined to the printed page.*

*Toni Davidson lives in Glasgow where he teaches English as a second language to bi-lingual children. We conversed via e-mail over several weeks.*

**STEVE REDHEAD** Your first edited collection *And Thus Will I Freely Sing* came out in 1989. What have you been doing between then and completing your novels?

**TONI DAVIDSON** After editing *And Thus Will I Freely Sing* I worked on performance readings at various Glasgow venues with a multimedia organisation called Flow, writing text to coincide with music, blurring it with the music – being the early nineties the text was both fervent and precious about hedonism and the right to party but some of it I think was okay and I can look back at it without cringing too much – it was a wonderful experience reading at volume. And the directness of the prose, the challenge to convert a written and fairly dense narrative was very satisfying – especially since I found little solace with London-based publishers. I worked collaboratively with other performance artists, meeting performers like Ron Athey and John Giorno. I also worked on short text installations with a production company called ISO, creating cut-up narratives that would be surrounded by graphics and then shown as part of an event. I also got involved with *Rebel Inc* when it was a magazine, reading at several of their events and at another spoken word collective called Yellow Moon Cafe. Here I got loads of support and mutual encouragement. It was a great time to be reading out work – people seemed to be interested in listening – far away from the usual pub reading. Even though I sometimes felt out on a limb from a fairly laddish/football culture I was made to feel part of what was happening. My subject matter, themes and in your face delivery was often rather different to those around me.

**S. R.** What were your 'literary' influences?

**T. D.** Literary influences?! A tough one – I can't name anyone that has had a direct influence on me to write. Literary osmosis is sometimes an intangible process but I love the Magic Realism of William Goyen, Texmex strangeness mixed up with passionate lyrical writing – stories about dreams or dreamlike existences juxtaposed with a degree of severity of the human condition – sorry bad syntax but this is my lunch hour! Also Paul Auster's dispassionate stories are something I love – the clinical, meticulous layering of stories, often inverting the linear narrative but again there is an incredible hook to his writing –

the theatre of coincidences, the tragedy of event sequences all stylised into an almost Pinteresque world. And also Jules Verne, possibly more of a recreational joy but the somewhat esoteric turn of phrase which can seem ridiculous now also seems to have the attraction of another world. I wrote my first novel when I was 17 – an unashamedly teenage story not a million miles away from SE Hinton's *The Outsiders* but I fell in love with Ponyboy – the kind of strong empathy which can be so important in the reader's reaction. I guess, to go back, in late teens Herman Hesse lured me into a world of attractive philosophy and fledging sexuality.

**S. R.** Can you tell me about your novels and your edited book on 'stimulant-based writing' *Intoxication?*

**T. D.** *Scar Culture* is my first (published) novel. Its themes are many I guess and describing what it's about is something I will have to get used to. It follows the stories of three characters Click, Fright and a pyschotherapy researcher Curtis Sad. Its issues range from experiences of interfamilial sexuality as described by all three characters to the experimental methodology used by Curtis Sad. I feel that although the book plays around with ideas of linear narrative and story accessibility its themes are fairly traditional – the survival of human qualities under intense pressures from horrific external factors, salvation from personal pain in intimacy with another (be that acceptable morally or not if it is a family member is a *big* question), the abuse of power and the exploitation for various reasons of another's pain. Click's narrative is the most straightforward – a lifestory told through photographs, headphotos and memory. Fright's character relates his story in an intense verbal staccatto via tape recordings and Curtis Sad and his counterpart in the USA (Wayne Peterson) hybrids officialese with his own erotic language and motivations. The book has three sections as well as a number of appendices – which I love to use – which add to the feeling that this book is a fictional document, a literary intervention as well as a novel. It isn't set anywhere in particular, there are no particular accents and there are maybe no more than three current cultural references. Is this not a trendy book? *Intoxication* on the other hand has been criticised by a *Times* critic for jumping on some kind of narco-lit bandwagon. As if! The book's idea was initiated more than five years ago. From my head it went to a meeting with Irvine Welsh and Barry Graham in Edinburgh and a few other writers who helped me build up a potential contributors list. I combined these with approaches to writers whose work I already liked – Gary Indiana, Elizabeth Young. And finally when the idea was accepted by Serpent's Tail I approached some of the writers (Lynne Tillman for example) who they had published. The manuscripts went through a number of line-ups but for a more detailed reasoning my introduction to the anthology kind of says all of it.

**S. R.** What popular cultural influences are there on your writing?

**T. D.** I find this quite a hard question to answer in that what I like by way of entertainment differs from what I want as stimulus to what I feel I want to write about. For instance I could read anything from Jules Verne to Paul Auster and not be able to find a sense of influence. But I guess what you are looking for is that for *Scar Culture* in particular I was absorbed by a book called *Making Monsters* which attempted to explode the myths surrounding recovered memories or at least tried to break through the hysteria and cynical manipulation by some therapists. In the same way I loved R.D. Laing's biography and found him a complex and brilliant stimulus. In *Scar Culture* I stayed clear of tagging any of the characters or narrative with icons or items of popular culture. It would have got in the way. It wasn't necessary to locate the book in that way in the mind of the reader. I couldn't write about football anyway. I couldn't write about a punk band anyway. It's just not me. Sometimes I feel as though I should be more up on what is around me and I guess I do try but I like timeless writing. Maybe that's an ambition – not to anchor my work in a particular decade. It's different with film. I can remember a scene from Philip Ridley's *The Reflecting Skin*, a lucid dream by the boy character that was both graphic and disturbing and the psychodrama placed before me stirred so much inside, dominoed associations and emotions that embedded themselves in my consciousness. If a film has gripped, has stirred me to the point that I do not want to leave the cinema, there's a good chance that there is a scene that I feel I can interpret and 'reissue'. These are woolly answers. I have loved cut-ups and I have loved Pinter dialogue – the cold emotional weight pressing down on my ears; the lurid melodrama of the whole of the film (and book) of *Erindrea*; the surreal juxtapositions and breaches of trust in the 10,000 fingers of Dr T. It all counts, whatever sears into the memory, carves its imprint etc. is what matters.

**S. R.** How far is gender part of what you and other 'new fiction' authors are writing about?

**T. D.** One aim with *Intoxication* was to re-establish the concept that stimulant-based writing can be observed as well as experienced by anyone. There seemed to be an imbalance in other collections where women's experience was not represented. That's not to say I was on some kind of Politically Correct (PC) crusade but it did seem to me that the anthology would be strengthened by diversity hence Richard Smith's piece or Bridget Connor's etc. Prior to *Scar Culture* a lot of my writing, particularly the story 'Young Hunks on Coke' (in *The Mammoth Book of Gay Short Stories* by Queer Words), dealt with gay men's experience outside of the scene and expected stereotypes and behaviour patterns. I saw Irvine Welsh's piece in the *Guardian* ('She's pregnant and he's got his fists raised: guess who's the victim . . .') on accusations against him of stereotyping, and I can't say I see a problem with his portrayal of women. I guess he's more interested in the entertainment of realism rather than adhering to liberal guidelines. Indeed the woman in 'A Soft Touch' (I forget her name) may not be a positive stencil for human behaviour but many women I spoke to from working-class backgrounds found her to be all too familiar. Having said that I'm not into mindless laddism and Irvine Welsh's writing is nowhere near that. I haven't actually got that much to add apart from to say that the 'new laddism' thing doesn't interest me that much. I feel I am on the margins of that one. I don't do most of the things 'new lads' are supposed to do. I'd rather read Dennis Cooper and absorb myself in the lives of fucked LA teenagers with permanent 'whatever' attitudes; his characters could be lads if they got old enough, straightened out and got British enough!

**S. R.** What link do you have to the gay community in Scotland, and elsewhere? How do you see contemporary gay politics?

**T. D.** Over the years I have been involved in organising literature events as part of gay festivals/gay strands within festivals namely 'Mayfest' 1989–1991 and 'Glasgay' '93 and '95. I used to edit the books for *Gay Scotland* magazine until about two years ago. Since starting *Scar Culture* I have had little to do with gay media aside from reviewing gay lit for *The List*. Apart from a few 'gay short stories' in *And Thus Will I Freely Sing*, 'The Crazy Jig' published by Polygon, 'Square Peg', 'A Queer Tribe' and 'Queer Words' I have not written a gay short story in quite a few years. This coincided with writing the unpublished *Weirdup* and the now published *Scar Culture*. I didn't have the time nor the inclination. I have always followed the Yves Navarre quotation 'I am gay, I am a writer, I am not a gay writer'. My interest in gay themes was limited just as I think so-called gay writing is in essence limited. All the gay writers that I liked – Genet, Baldwin, White, Michael Cunningham, Dennis Cooper to name a few – extended the themes of their writing wider than the usual coming out/gay scene-type stories. I felt I wanted to explore themes and interests beyond the niche I could have carved out for myself. I am not sure people can tell *Scar Culture* was written by a gay man and I am happy with that. I am not in denial about my sexuality but I will resist categorisation and fixed labels. Pansexuality in terms of gay politics has always been something to believe in and interestingly I don't think that is seen as such a political cop-out as it used to be – see the recent article by Peter Tatchell in the *Guardian*. There is a political need for gays' sexuality to be recognised but a personal desire not to be assimilated into one particular group. The fight for gay rights is a fight for human rights. Have Amnesty International got that message? I hope so.

**S. R.** What involvement do you still have in clubcultures?

**T. D.** I still love my decks, more so now that I actually seem to be able to mix! But I was always more nervous DJ-ing than I was reading and I would only do it at parties or in an environment that wasn't too full of people I knew! I still club but I guess with a discerning eye, which is usually, I know, what people say as they get older. The end result is that I am now going to jazz nights or hip hop nights, a welcome change after years of techno and house. Club culture itself has changed with the ravers becoming club dancers again and this demise of the large-scale free parties is only for club-owners' benefit – all under one roof is not the same as one nation under a groove. But lamenters of those lost raves are in danger of sounding like the hippies so many people are disdainful of. What is passé for one generation is the start of something fresh for a new generation. Also, I still work with graphic designers ISO based in Glasgow, making short prose work for showing in a club environment – messages mixed with graphics then shown on slides or video projectors. I worked as a researcher on a Blackwatch Production called *Sub 18* about under-18 clubbing in Glasgow to be shown on Channel 4 at some point.

**S. R.** Can you tell me about your next novel *Wild Justice*?

**T. D.** *Wild Justice* is a provisional title. It concerns itself with an agency (of that name) for non-violent revenge where people come to the organisation with specific needs and the employees carry out action on their behalf. The novel, like *Scar Culture*, has a split narrative where the four characters and their reasons for being in 'Wild Justice' are sliced together. As much as it concentrates on the workings of the agency, it also deals with its competition with on-line revenge outfits, as well as the violent hitmen agencies. It also delves into the reasons for, and the moral dilemmas about, 'getting even'. Its four characters Shoal Wake, Silem Renk, Mela Vich and Effem Leesh tell their own story and each section starts along a different part of the time line, so 'linear' is kind of played around with. For example, Silem Renk journeys back to visit John Tillotson, a Dean of Canterbury in the late seventeenth century famous for his anti-revenge standpoint, while Shoal Wake is a hip-talking, wise-cracking foot soldier for revenge who apparently has no moral problem with it. The novel is more ambitious than *Scar Culture* in the sense that I want to layer it even more and provide the narrative with the same intense character impact – they all have to have strong voices. But it will be a 'lighter' book. I feel the voices in my head when I write will be diverse, giving me opportunity for black comedy – my favourite genre!

*Roddy Doyle*

# New Island
## Roddy Doyle

*Roddy Doyle was born in Dublin in the late 1950s and is author of*
The Commitments, The Van, The Snapper, Paddy Clarke Ha Ha Ha,
The Woman Who Walked Into Doors *and* A Star Called Henry. *He
contributed an Eire football fan memoir to Nick Hornby's collection* My
Favourite Year *and a Chelsea fan memoir to* Perfect Pitch.

*The* Barrytown Trilogy *– his first three novels of Dublin working-class
culture – have all been filmed. Alan Parker filmed* The Commitments
*whilst Stephen Frears filmed* The Snapper *and* The Van. *He has written
two plays,* Brownbread *and* War, *and the TV series* Family. *His fourth
novel* Paddy Clarke Ha Ha Ha *won the Booker Prize. Even after
completing his first two novels Roddy Doyle was still teaching English
and Geography at a school in north Dublin.*

*His name has become something of a byword in new fiction.
For instance, Duncan McLean, who began the Clocktower Press,
was described as 'Scotland's answer to Roddy Doyle' when his first
novels appeared and younger Irish writers like Neville Thompson are
labelled 'Roddy Doyle with knobs on'. The* Commitments *was initially
self-published by Doyle and John Sutton in 1987 and they hoped to
attract and publish other fiction from outside the literary establishment:
none materialised. In the decade that followed, as this present book
reveals, new or cult fiction eventually prospered. Some of it indeed
developed in Ireland as hip, younger writers reacted against the new
media 'stereotypes' of Irish culture.*

*Roddy Doyle is currently writing a new trilogy based on his fiction-
alised view of Irish history.* A Star Called Henry *is the first of these
three books to be published. He lives in Dublin where we talked in the
offices of John Sutton (now his manager), just across from the Temple
Bar area.*

**STEVE REDHEAD** Why did you write fiction? Why did you start?

**RODDY DOYLE** I think because I read so much. And given the choice between say watching a fictional film – a feature film – and a documentary I suppose nine times out of ten I'd go for the feature film. In most cases they tend to be better made. They were more engrossing. There were some outstanding documentary films I'd seen on the big screen but the bulk of films were fiction. And I liked fiction when I was a kid. And a teenager. And I began to realise that a great book was written by a human being who may have written other books and I began to follow them. So I suppose it was taste really as much as anything else. Or accident. Ignorance would maybe come into it as well. Because obviously as you got older you realise there's only twenty-four hours in a day and time is running out. So I suppose because I liked fiction I ended up writing it. Also I don't think I write very quickly. Over the years I've produced work regularly but I don't write quickly. I don't have the type of mind that works well under pressure. So if I'd been drawn towards say journalism, if I'd accepted some of the offers that were given to me as my first books were published, I think it would have been a disaster. The idea of even going to a football match and then reporting back on it immediately, which is a trivial enough thing to do, would crease me. It just doesn't suit me at all. Whereas writing fiction, it can be quite intense, it has its own pressures, but generally time isn't one of them. So I have the luxury of time. A good day's work can often be a page. There were times when I was writing *The Woman Who Walked Into Doors* when it was a paragraph. I could devote my time to it. Later on it began to flow better. But I suppose with experience I began to realise that making up stories suits me down to the ground. And I find I can do something that's authentic in that way. Whereas going out into the world and observing and coming back and reporting wouldn't probably suit me.

I have done little bits and pieces of 'journalism' always responding to invitations and ninety-nine times out of a hundred I've said no. The *My Favourite Year* piece, it just struck me. I admire Nick Hornby anyway, it was him that got in touch with me and he asked me would I do it. And I just thought it was such a glorious month in Ireland that

I thought I will try and capture it and use, if you like, the same sort of passion that I put into the fiction. But I wouldn't be interested in going around looking for opportunities – besides which I did so much drinking in that month that I couldn't possibly survive if I decided to write like that! Going into bull rings, you know, pissed as a rat!! I just recently did one though for a bi-annual magazine called *Perfect Pitch* – I think it will be out in 1999 – about my son's growing infatuation with football. Again the invitation came and I thought 'yeah, this is where I could capture this moment in his life'. That's all there was to it. But I wouldn't be interested again in going around looking for excuses. I really love it, at this stage now, the type of thing I'm doing, I love doing the research, delving into subjects. At the moment I'm reading about Louis Armstrong and becoming more and more fascinated and worked up about the man and listening to the music and driving myself into a position where I can start writing about him and creating a fictional version of him if you like. And fictional people and real people around him. I find that really really engrossing, probably more so than meeting a real musician and coming home and writing about him.

I've just finished one of the novels – in this new trilogy – and it will be out in September 1999. It's the first of what will probably be three books. It's about this man who was born in 1902. And it follows his life. He's narrating his life and it goes from 1902 to 1922 when he goes out of Ireland. So I'm now working myself up into starting the second volume. I want to have started the second volume before the first book comes out. Louis Armstrong is just an idea. Like a lot of the diehard Republicans are people who got in trouble during the war of independence and they ended up in the States and a lot of them ended up in Chicago and there was a review of a biography of Louis Armstrong that got this idea into my head. Now I haven't finally decided yet – I have to do more. There are other ideas which aren't compatible. I'm at the stage where I'm looking at them all over the place. And if I decide on one idea I have to drop about five. I'm just trying to plot out. I don't plan too carefully or too meticulously because I don't think I'd write if I had everything planned too meticulously. A lot of the fun and more importantly a lot of the anxiety which seems to be quite important would disappear and it would become too lacklustre or something, I don't know.

**S. R.**  Who were your influences – in the fiction that you read?

**R. D.**  *The Commitments* was the first published novel. I spent four years writing another novel which will never be published. I think I actually rather pompously put it down on paper and signed that this book must never be published. It took me four years and the title is the best thing about it: *Your Granny's A Hunger Striker* and it goes badly downhill after that. It does if I remember – I wouldn't be able to read it now. It's very long, very big, a tedious thing, set around Dublin in the summer of 1981 with a whole gang of characters. It really doesn't work. But I do think that there are moments in it which are very funny. I look back on it now and quite neatly think of it as my apprenticeship when I began to realise what you can and can't do. I started *The Commitments* immediately after finishing this in 1986. *The Commitments* took about six months. About half of it I wrote in the Easter break. I stayed up all night writing. Because that's what I thought you were supposed to do. When I was a teenager the names that hit me were Flann O'Brien and Joseph Heller. They were the names that really hit me between the eyes when I was about seventeen in particular. Flann O'Brien was a group activity really – a bit like discovering alcohol and women. There was a group of us used to sit, it was a glorious sunmmer in 1975 I think, and we kind of sat under a tree on Saturday nights reading *The Third Policeman* out loud. To outsiders we must have been a tedious bunch of people. But to us it was just hilarious. I think writing the first novel probably got Flann O'Brien out of my system, that attempt to emulate him and copy him, which is virtually impossible. And Joseph Heller then. *Catch 22* if I remember rightly was the only one that was published at that time. *Something Happened* then came out. I hadn't started looking at book reviews then – hardback books out of the question. I'd have read *Something Happened* when it came out in paperback and it was very disappointing. I suspect I would enjoy it much more if I read it again now, and then *Good As Gold* followed soon after that. But it was interesting seeing a living author and his career on the move. And so they spring to mind.

I went to University then (University College Dublin) and I was doing my own independent reading and other authors started to catch my attention, Flannery O'Connor, people like that. Later on Anne Tyler and Raymond Carver. You know, fairly obvious people, not necessarily that they had an influence on what I do, but I don't think in those terms when I'm following a career of a writer. I don't think in terms of what can they give me. It's more whether I enjoy it or not, whether I think the writing's really good or not. George V. Higgins was another writer I really admired and Elmore Leonard was very special. So they're the ones that spring to mind. I did read *On The Road* which I enjoyed a lot but I found it a little tedious at times. But then when I found out about him going home to write the book at his mammy's house I found that quite comforting. It's not the fault of the writers but the legends that are around them. Bukowski's a great writer, I really love him. And I love his world even though I wouldn't want to live in it. It's the mythology then, this idea that you can't be a writer unless you're a hard-living drunkard, you can't be a writer unless you go on the road, you have to experience. This writes off most people's experience, not just my own but everybody's, this rule of thumb that you must write what you know. If it's taken very broadly and it includes the imagination – grand. But if it's taken literally and it often is, it's a crime to actually try and inflict that on anybody who wants to write. I do think the legends of Hemingway and Kerouac and people like that, through no fault of their own I think have done damage. I'm sure you have met journalists you know who do cooking reviews who really feel that they are actually Ernest Hemingway. That's what it is to be a writer – to pose, to sit in the right pub, wear the right clothes and be suitably foul-mouthed when drunk. I think it takes a while to get away from that and to be comfortable with yourself and to let your imagination run riot, rather than yourself run riot. If you want to run riot yourself – grand. But it's not part of the package.

**S. R.** What about popular cultural influences on your writing?

**R. D.** I suppose to an extent in *The Commitments* having decided I wanted to bring a gang of young people – kids whatever – together there were two obvious things I remember thinking about at the time.

One was a football team and one was a band. And I had a great friend called Paul Mercia who had written this brilliant play called *Studs* which my manager John Sutton produced actually, and it was about a team, a hopeless Sunday morning football team, and it was just a superb play. It was great fun. It was like ballet at times, little action replays, it just played with the whole video thing. And I felt that was the perfect place for it, either watching real football on the telly or this choreographed great thing. But I've never actually enjoyed reading blow by blow accounts of a football match. Even Sunday morning papers, I don't like reading accounts of matches unless I'd seen them myself and they're well written. So I didn't see much scope for it. I saw much more scope in the music. Then rooting around, I was listening to a lot of soul music at the time, and I'd read Peter Guralnick's books and the characters if you like, these are real people, but James Brown and the guys in the Stax studios they really grabbed me. I loved the idea of getting some of their energy and their ideas and to an extent their cynicism in one or two cases into a bunch of Dublin guys like Jimmy Rabitte. I thought the scope for humour was great. And the band was going to be bigger. The scope for bullshit philosophy was there as well. Then writing out the lyrics and trying to make the rhythm of the text fit the rhythm of the lyrics and even the drumbeat – dum bududum – I spent ages on these drumbeats, oh god almighty, and listening to the same lines of the song again and again. So I suppose really the music imposed the style.

Of all the books I've written *The Snapper* is probably the one that's least polluted by music – there's not much music in it at all but I was more consciously aware, I suppose it's the difficult second album idea, more consciously aware of rhythm and how a badly placed comma can make you trip over. I spent ages on the rhythm of the book, knitting the dialogue with the narrative and trying to make sure that at moments of excitement there were short bursts and more reflective moments. I suppose it's standard. But I was more consciously aware of listening to the music of the words in my head, taking out a word that had one too many syllables and putting in another one so it would all knit. The more recent books have been packed with music. I listen to music that I think will inspire me. The last book, there was a piece of music by Philip Glass. There were two pieces of music I listened to for the rhythm more than anything else when I was writing the last book, particularly in the afternoon when time was running out and I was wanting to get a day's work done. There was one piece by Philip Glass which is literally an hour long and if you listen to it casually there's no change. It's not like his later work which I like too – I think it's 1971 or something he composed it – and it's very abstract and you have to listen inside it to hear the slight changes along the way. But the rhythm of it is something I've never heard before and it really got my fingers tapping when I was writing. Now I was writing about Ireland in 1919 – Philip Glass I don't think would be familiar with that. Another thing that got me working was 'After Extra Time', a piece by Michael Nyman, which is about football, but you don't have to know that to appreciate it. It's glorious pounding music going on and on and on and because there are no lyrics to interfere with one's concentration that really got into me and again got my fingers working away. A day after listening to 'After Extra Time' it was very productive, not necessarily in terms of the quality – I can go back and fix that – but in terms of quantity it dragged a good extra page or two pages out of me. I think as part of growing up – I'm not sure – like a lot of people I started listening to classical music as well, one of the reasons being that I wanted to listen to music while I worked. Having worked as a teacher for fourteen years being surrounded by flushing toilets and running feet and screaming teachers I was suddenly in a position where I had only two children and they were both in the créche during the daytime so I was in an empty house. I quite like the noise – I live near a hospital for example, and it's not that one is ghoulish but I don't mind the noise of the siren. I live near Dublin airport, I can handle the noise. I thought, here I am, I've got eight hours during the day to myself, it seems a shame while I'm writing also not to try to listen to music. I couldn't listen to pop and rock – it's too distracting – so I started to listen to classical music and I think that a lot of people listen to classical music on the radio coming home from work and for want of a better phrase 'get into it'. And I've also recently started listening to quite a lot of jazz although there's so much music within that it's an unsatisfactory description of the word 'jazz'. But I've started actually delving in there as well. Having the time during the day to listen but also I suppose – although there's some great music being created – a general dissatisfaction with the current state of rock and pop music, too many people just delving through the old *Top of the Pops* and finding great disco hits from 1973 and putting a different beat on it and then releasing it. It's a bit tedious. It was shite in 1973 and sometimes it's slightly better shite now because it's a bit cooler, but it's still shite!!

**S. R.**  Were you actually taught to write in any way?

**R. D.**  No, I did English Literature at University. But I read. There were one or two teachers who would have an influence but because of their encouragement not because they said 'you should do that or that'. I'm talking about one of them which was when I was in fourth class, when I was about nine or ten. There were two teachers who I can think back on who sort of patted me on the back and said that's very good. I grew up in an era in education when that was relatively rare. So I'd always remember them with a lot of affection. But other than that I think it's just all the reading I did. One of the good things about *The Commitments* when it was released here was that people either loved it or hated it. There was a lot of hostility to the first three books and there still is in Dublin and in Ireland generally. There's two ways you can cope with that. It can either knock you down or you can develop an arrogance and I think I did develop an arrogance or a confidence in what I do, an absolute certainty. I think I'm a good editor of my own work and a good judge of my own work. I think a lot of the bad reviews helped to an extent. After a while when I read them I realised they were bad bad reviews if you know what I mean – they were just badly written; they were people with grudges. There was one great thing about *The Commitments* – a lot of people in the music press detested *The Commitments*, how it was so dishonest and nothing to do with music and who was this guy? A year after it was published Elvis Costello wrote an article for an anniversary edition of *Hot Press* where he said that *The Commitments* was very accurate, it was like living through *The Commitments* when he put his first band on the road. I thought 'great, who said I knew nothing about music'! And then Rory Gallagher, God rest him, he also said it. This was terrific. It was a great boost to my confidence. The journalists, who somehow think because they review albums they're musicians, or because they wear the same clothes they're musicians, were rubbishing what I'd done and then the real musicians came out and said it was good. It gave me a lot of self-confidence. I wasn't interested in accuracy really, I never have been. With the exception of the last book *The Woman Who Walked Into Doors* where every word had to be true as the subject matter. I'm quite happy to warp reality, to break it and put it together again if it suits the book. You do it with film, you know, you try to capture a life in a feature film that lasts an hour and a half, you go into the editing booth and snip it, you do the exact same thing in writing except it's not as glaringly obvious, it's not as manipulated I suppose. But it is to a degree, it's just not as dramatic because there's only one person at the keyboard or writing out, whereas with film you've got whole loads of people and you can have any amount of different cuts. With writing it's the exact same, and I have no problem whatsoever taking short cuts with reality. I didn't really care whether 'The Commitments' was a real live band or not, I just thought within the covers of the book if it was feasible, if it seemed believable, that was fine by me.

**S. R.** Did you have a direct input into the way that the films were done?

**R. D.** For *The Commitments* I co-wrote the screenplay, so that's as direct as I got. I wasn't involved in day-to-day. I stayed away actually. And I did like it. I haven't seen it since it was released. I saw cuts so often and it became such a media legend here in Ireland that it began to bore me, and worry me and I wondered whether I'd be the 'person who wrote *The Commitments*' for the rest of my life. I remember watching it and I was quite nervous and I hadn't been around to see any of it filmed so I didn't know what I was going to see. About twenty minutes into the film I began to relax. I thought it was very, very good. It stayed very close to the spirit; that was more important than a blow by blow. I've adapted my own work since. I've been working on an adaptation of Liam O'Flaherty's novel *Famine* and it's a question of trying to get the money, trying to persuade people to give you the money to tell a story in a film about peasants starving to death – the MTV possibilities are fairly slim you know! So what you do is try to keep the spirit of the thing. What works on paper often doesn't work on screen. I think it was into the second and third drafts of *Famine* I was sort of getting rid of characters that are glorious in the novel but just clutter the screenplay. It's something I never thought I would have done. I find it no problem at all doing it with my own work. But trying to do it with someone else's work, even though he's dead, one has to be respectful but the spirit of the thing is more important than the absolute page by page accuracy.

I think, of the others, the film of *The Snapper* would be my favourite. I'm also fond of *The Van*. At the moment I don't think there's a big enough distance between *The Van* being made and released and now for me to have a more objective thing. *The Van* I was more involved with. *The Snapper* I was still teaching. It was frustrating because there was a lot of the filming going on literally on the street outside the school and I was teaching fucking geography – the rivers and mountains of Ireland – when something far more interesting was going on outside. So I didn't see as much as I'd have liked. Whereas with *The Van* I was there every day and I did quite a lot of rewriting, I enjoyed it. Then I went over to London every Wednesday virtually to see the latest cut, so I was right there bang in front of it. I felt very much as if it was my baby even though it was group affair. So I was very protective of it. I don't feel qualified yet to say whether I prefer it to *The Snapper*. I enjoy them very much. I was very moved by *The Van* the first time I saw it. Now whether I would when I go to look at it again I don't know. The last book *The Woman Who Walked Into Doors* I don't think would translate into film. It's not impossible I suppose but the inspiration for writing the novel came from writing a television script for the BBC in the first place – this was *Family* – and having written the television story and then writing the novel because I wanted to get closer to the character and describe her experience, I had the freedom to go back into her past and forward a couple of years and get into her head. I know I wouldn't want to do a film about it. There is an opera of *The Commitments* being done by a Belgian company – which is what normally I wouldn't do

– because it was more interesting than a lot of other things. Virtually every week I have to say no to the latest request to do a musical of *The Commitments* – it just has no appeal to me whatsoever. Whereas I just thought this was so novel. I've been to a couple of operas. The story lines are desperate, even though the arias can be glorious. I just thought what are they going to do with this? The only way you're going to find out is to let them do it. I think it's to be ready in the year 2000.

*Paddy Clarke* possibly could be a film. At the time when it was published I felt I didn't want to know. Then it won the Booker Prize and suddenly every producer in the world wanted the rights. Once word is out that you've done a new book, people who've never read the book, they just want it. That's something you have to be very wary of. They have no problem enthusing about something. It's just when you ask them a couple of questions you realise that they're not in any way involved. Even a few people who've read the *Famine* screenplay and they've been warned 'this is set in 1845, it's about people starving to death' and they flick through it looking for the jokes! 'Where do they sing Mustang Sally?' You have to fight your own stereotype. I think *Paddy Clarke* could make a good film but it would take a lot of work. Whereas with the first three novels you had a linear plot there for you anyway and you could hang your script on it. With *Paddy Clarke* it would be easy enough to break it down and assemble it again in a different fashion. On a practical note I'd be terrified about putting a year's work into the script and being unable to find a kid who could carry the part. I was delighted with *Family*, particularly the last episode which was the trickiest because it was the least dramatic. Much of the controversy was caused by the first episode here in Ireland – all sorts of people giving out about it – but the final episode was the least controversial, it was just about a woman surviving. I thought it was brilliant. It had a huge impact here, it was quite an unsettling one. To put it in print as a screenplay it would need a bit of work, it would need tidying up, perhaps an introduction. Although I work a five day week, Monday to Friday, going back on old things? I prefer to just push forward, write a new page of a novel, work on a new script. I find it very difficult to motivate myself, even though I'm really happy with the *Family* script.

But I found then when I talked to students about the *Family* script that I'd end up talking about sociology with them which is not the literature, it's not the rhythm of the speech that they were interested in at all and I'm wary of that because I'm nobody's expert on anything, except my own work perhaps, and even then there are people who are far more familiar with the work because once I've finished I don't tend to read it. And there are some people who are doing a thesis or a dissertation who know the books far better than I do.

**S. R.** Were you conscious when you were writing that so much of your fiction is about masculinity?

**R. D.** At this stage I don't know whether you can say that. You can probably get the scales out and measure it. I am a man after all so I am limited by that. But I mean *The Woman Who Walked Into Doors*, from what I've been told by women who read it, captured the experience of the woman. *The Snapper* was as much about a woman as a man. I tried to actually walk two lines there, to have the crude world of the pub and the 'woman's world' as well. It took a good while to write because of that. I've always tried to include women, it's no problem at all about writing about women. My latest book is very much a man's book. Even the people who have read it, the response from men has been far wilder, if you like, than women even though women have liked it – it seems to be more of a man's book. I have no need to apologise for that, I reckon it's just this particular book that suits it. When I wrote *The Commitments* I don't think that there was one female band around at the time except maybe there was the group from Los Angeles who had a couple of hits before they broke up. But women's involvement in music was very much limited to singing and looking good frankly. If I was writing *The Commitments* now I would probably be more adventurous in terms of its make up, but maybe not, because the bulk of bands are still four young men, three young men. There are wankers out there who probably if I wrote about a football team would say 'you've no women'. There was actually an alternative distribution company here who refused to distribute *The Commitments* because it was 'sexist' and it was 'sexist' because there were only two women in the band, none of them played instruments, and the book said that it was 'more important how they looked than how they sang'. A character in the book said that. And even *The Van* which is very much an unemployed man's story, his wife is a very important presence in that book. *Paddy Clarke*? What can you say? It's about a boy. I suppose if I'd written only the first three novels there might be something of interest there – but you can go to the work of most male writers who've been writing for the last thousand years and you can throw that barb at them.

**S. R.** What about new up and coming Irish fiction writers? Is there a Dublin, or Irish subculture of writers of new fiction?

**R. D.** I think Mike McCormack – he's attracted a lot of attention for the short story collection *Getting It in the Head*, which is fantastic. It came out of the same place as John McGahern's short stories geographically or whatever, but it was a different world entirely. McGahern is a superb writer. McCormack's stories are well written stories, very funny stories. It was almost a new place entirely that he was writing about, I liked that. His novel *Crowe's Requiem* was disappointing.

I was under the impression for a long time that literary Dublin was very snooty, that I was not approved of by literary Dublin. I didn't know what literary Dublin was. I discovered that it was actually two journalists in the *Irish Times* who were dictating this and that they were not altogether accurate either. I notice that in their books of the year this year they both went for the same three, including John Updike's book which is really quite tedious. I didn't know any writers other than this playwright friend of mine who hasn't written fiction. It's a revelation to meet them all because they are all very supportive. There's a certain amount of bitching but far less than there was in the world of teaching, much less, far far less.

There's no such thing, as far as I know, as a literary pub. I mean there are gangs of people who meet, but there's no round table or anything like that. As far as I know a phone call and just being mutually supportive is quite common. Mike McCormack, I've never met him but certainly I thought the collection of stories was great. Dermot Healy I admire enormously. I like the work of Joe O'Connor. I suppose you get down to talking about individual books after a while.

I thought Joe's last novel was terrific, really very, very good. Basically the bulk of writers who are living and writing in Dublin would wish one well. A lot of that hostility that one was led to believe was there in fact wasn't. I published *The Commitments* myself, it was my one and only publication. At the time myself and John Sutton let it be known that if we got manuscripts that we really liked we'd have a bash and do it again but unfortunately nothing arrived. Reality began to encroach – John had this other job, I was teaching, we just didn't have the time to be publishers as well. Dermot Bolger has done great work, leaving aside his work as a novelist, with his New Island press – it used to be Raven Arts – he's given most of the major poets that have emerged a start. It's a Dublin based company, they've done a lot of exciting work in fiction and poetry over the years. It gave a lot of people a kick start.

*John King*

# **Millennial Man**

John King

*John King was born in the 1960s and comes from London. He is author of the loose fiction trilogy* The Football Factory, Headhunters *and* England Away. *He contributed the short story 'Space Junk' to the* Intoxication *collection and 'The Beasts of Marseille' to* Fortune Hotel.

The Football Factory *has been dramatised for the stage and sold over 200,000 copies as a first novel.* Headhunters *is being scripted for a film. Dave Hill, writing in the* Observer *coined the term 'Millennium Men' – a mixture of 'New Lad' and 'New Man' – for the target of advertising and marketing around football culture. John King's fiction, drawing on his long experience as a Chelsea fan, gives a picture of 'Millennial Man' not readily available elsewhere.*

*John King had his own London based underground fanzine called* Two Sevens *in the early 1990s and also published a one-off literature pamphlet called* Verbal. *In the 'fiction with attitude' issue of* Verbal *which came out about the same time as* Rebel Inc *Issue 5 in the mid-1990s writers like* Rebel Inc *favourite Laura Hird were featured alongside English stalwarts like Attila the Stockbroker and Stewart Home. The strength of this small 'underground' literary press was partly that it gave sustenance to writers who were outside the middle-class literary establishment; based in London and heavily Oxbridge influenced. As a result a different kind of fiction began to be published, written by younger people who would previously have been huffily regarded as 'outsiders' or 'deviant' writers.*

*John King is completing his fourth novel* Human Punk. *I talked with him at his flat in London surrounded by his records, books and computer and he later sent me written answers to some further questions I wanted to ask.*

**STEVE REDHEAD** What influence did punk have on you? What effect did it have on your fiction?

**JOHN KING** Probably it's age and that. Me and Kevin Williamson and Irvine Welsh are in our thirties now. We were kids when punk was about. In a lot of ways I'd say that we're from that. You know, techno is a continuation of that for a different generation. A lot of people who had sound systems used to be punks, so I think there's a link even if there aren't the lyrics of punk, maybe we're the ones supplying the words now. It came from music definitely. When I was young there was very little literature that had anything to do with my life. When I was a teenager, when I was fourteen or fifteen, I had a Ziggy Stardust haircut, DM's and we called ourselves boot boys and went in the Shed in Chelsea. I read the [Richard Allen] *Skinhead* books because that's all there was. Some of my reviews say 'he writes like the *Skinhead* books' but that's rubbish, the whole stance is different, the style is different. The bloke who wrote the *Skinhead* books wrote them in one day. There's a lot of things in there that are offensive I think. You know, when I was a kid I didn't know what rape was but I still knew that the fact that Joe Hawkins was raping a woman and she was supposed to enjoy it was bollocks. I did read them, along with the Mick Norman and *Confessions* books, but what really influenced me was punk especially The Clash and Pistols. The Clash for their politics, the Pistols for their attitude. And also Sham 69. I thought Jimmy Pursey's idea that you should really go into the lion's den rather than preaching to the converted, I always thought he was really spot on with that. And he was slagged off by the music press left, right and centre. But he was brave. In a lot of ways he was braver than the other bands who were playing to people who totally agreed with what they said.

So I took most of my education from punk and by punk I mean the ideas and music, not the bondage gear and funny haircuts. We were 'herberts' really. I read Orwell and Huxley and American writers like Hubert Selby Jnr. I really respect those people. Orwell's essays are still true today. I read Kerouac and Charles Bukowski when I was fifteen or something. I think the 'Beat' writers were interesting because they were trying to create something different, but having said that they were bankrolled by their mums and dads. Burroughs came from a very rich family, Kerouac was always getting money off his mum. The idea was good but the actual content, I thought, was quite weak. I prefer writers like Hubert Selby Jnr who is much harder. I think with the American writers there's not the same class system, so people were coming through and doing new things which I don't think Britain's really had. Certainly nothing on the American scale. So since I was nineteen I wanted to write but it was always off in the future.

**S. R.** Did punk fanzines influence you? Or, later, football fanzines?

**J. K.** I suppose it was, I don't know, maybe the people who were doing the fanzines were a few years older than me, I was still at school. I was fifteen, sixteen. No, I didn't do that síde of it. I think with writing a lot of it for me was having the discipline. I think when you're young you don't really – or I didn't – have that discipline. I was going to see bands and I was into football in a big way. You'd be down the pub five or six nights a week, working Monday to Friday, and at football on Saturday, so you didn't really have the time to do it. But it was always in my head, it just wasn't a priority. When I got to thirty, I thought if I'm going to do something, I've got to make the effort now. But it was always sort of there. When I was about twenty I worked in this warehouse and did some writing – when I wanted to be George Orwell – because it was pretty quiet and they used to have this little place at the back where I could hide, and write stuff. I did that for a few months but I never really took it on from there.

In the mid-eighties I had the idea of doing something on football. The way Thatcher was making football out to be was wrong as far as I saw things. So I thought I'd write something but again I never really had the time or discipline. So it was always in my mind and with the fanzine (*Two Sevens*) it was just sort of something me and my mate Pete talked about doing for ages. But I think in some ways it was harder because it was the early nineties when we did *Two Sevens* and people would have an eighty-pound leather jacket but wouldn't have a pound for a magazine. I had 'Millwall Away' published in *Rebel Inc* around this time. It was just good luck that I found *Rebel Inc* in Compendium bookshop. We were looking for small press material to review. It was just something we found, maybe on the fourth issue we just came across it. I think fanzines are good because they're fresh. People do them for love. When money becomes involved they join the mainstream and lose their edge. It's like when *When Saturday Comes* came out, mid-eighties wasn't it, I've probably still got some, like the fourth issue with sixteen pages. They were good. I can remember lending them to someone who had a party round his house, the place was full of blokes sitting there reading them, thinking this is really good. But then it changed, like anything; people see they can get a career on the *Guardian* or something and so it changes and it becomes part of the establishment. It happens to everything I think.

There's a bloke who used to do *Skinhead Times* called George Marshall, and he redid all the *Skinhead* books and set up his own little publishing outfit doing books on ska and skinhead culture. He's doing a street-punk paper called *Pulped* now. He's stayed true to his ideals. I've never met him but I've corresponded with him. Skinhead culture isn't how it is shown today. It came out of Jamaican culture, it was a black thing. It was the first acceptance in Britain. I would say that the first acceptance of immigration in the sixties was skinheads and curry houses. No middle-class people went to curry houses twenty years ago. The people who kept them going were blokes out on the piss. It's the same with ska. If you talk to older blokes who are in their fifties now, they say everyone was listening to ska music. It's interesting. A lot of that history gets airbrushed. Even like my Dad. He grew up in Hounslow and they were listening to boogie-woogie records in the late thirties, early forties. They were listening to black music during the war.

What else did we come across? There was one called *Dog*, which was a poetry pamphlet, there was Kevin Williamson's stuff, there was George Marshall's ST Publishing. And Duncan McLean's *Clocktower Press*. There was this massive fanzine called *Wake Up* by a bloke called Dave T. It had everything in it, from music to politics. It was a yearly thing and I think there's another due soon. We came across a lot of rubbish as well – students telling the world how right on they were but at least they were doing it themselves. I love all that.

**S. R.**  Why and how did you get into writing fiction?

**J. K.**  I think that the small scale press is maybe where you get your confidence up. And also I didn't know anyone who wrote. I'd never met a writer. And getting to know Kevin Williamson, because we were both doing something, was good because he'd give me a view on what I was writing. And that was very encouraging. I got friendly with Stewart Home through *Two Sevens*. I think he's a great writer, very underrated. He's his own man. Obeys no rules. I've known him for a few years now. The only fiction I had published before *The Football Factory* book was 'Millwall Away' in *Rebel Inc*. I'd had the idea for *The Football Factory* and I started writing it in the early 1990s and I did a load and I looked at it and thought 'this is rubbish, you've got to think about how you're going to write and people do say fuck and cunt, I say fuck and cunt, so you've got to write it down no matter what your mum says.' Once you make that decision you become more honest I think. Then I went on from there. I didn't have to do any research – but it's fiction, I'm not the character. But I have been going to football for a long time. I think you can do more with fiction. I wanted to write fiction from the start. That's the main thing. I don't think I'd be disciplined enough to be a reporter or factual writer. You can make more points in fiction. You have more freedom writing about a fictional character. You can make a lot of points in more direct ways. Basically I want to be a fiction writer. I think that's really what it's about, to create characters, look at society. To me my books aren't really about football. There's older characters in my books. To me the soldier in *England Away* is the most important character.

The trilogy was my idea. I think what it was, I wrote *The Football Factory* first of all and then I had the idea for *Headhunters* which wasn't to do with football. As I was going into them I found I wanted to write more and more about the characters. It took over in a way. A lot of characters that you introduce you want to do more with them. I think with *England Away* it sort of felt right to do it. It would be overseas and it would be looking at the idea of being English. The thing with the old boy, 'we don't do that sort of stuff'. He is an honourable man and that's what happens in that sort of situation. The publishers never really pushed me in the football direction. They've been really good. Robin Robertson is really sound. He knows nothing about football. He took me on as a writer. When he makes a comment at first you might not like it but I respect his view. He's honest. *The Football Factory* came out in 1996 and they accepted it the year before, 1995. I sent it to them originally in 1994. When I first sent it Robin rejected it and said 'you'll have to do more work on it but it's better than a lot of stuff I get so keep me in mind.' Then I did some short stories and then I went back to *The Football Factory*. So it was 1995 they accepted it. I had ten pounds in the bank and the clutch had gone on my 1982 Ford Sierra. I couldn't do more than 20mph up a hill. He phoned up and said 'can you come in' and I went to Cape and he said he wanted to publish it – brilliant! I really think that if it wasn't for Robin being open-minded enough to do a different sort of literature nobody else would have, not even the small trendy publishers. They definitely wouldn't have done it because they're more interested in 'alternative' sex and drugs in Oxford and Cambridge. If it wasn't for Robin I don't think *Trainspotting* would have been published either.

**S. R.**  What and who influenced you in writing?

**J. K.**  I mean I always had it in my head as well for years that there should be a literature that is contemporary, relevant, energetic, instead of rows and rows of dull university lectures, same as they have in America. The best sort of contemporary American novel is Bret Easton Ellis' *American Pyscho*. I think that is a brilliant book. I mean I haven't read any of Bret Easton Ellis' others and I probably wouldn't want to. That's a good book. He knows that scene – he's from it. At the same time he's been able to write about it honestly. He doesn't care if people slag him off. I couldn't have done that, I wouldn't know the labels or anything about 'yuppies'. So I always thought it was there to do. Why should a small percentage of people write about the same thing again and again and have all this space on the bookshelves? There's so many different types of people in this country. You could have literature from London, Bristol, Leeds, Manchester, Cardiff – you could have rural stuff – there's so much scope really.

But I think being English is harder, certainly in a lot of ways, than being Scottish. The Scots, the Gaelic people, have got a culture of story-telling. It's not considered effeminate to write books, whereas if you're English it's different. I think also that the media give you a rougher ride because you're sort of on their doorstep. If you're writing in London slagging off the people who run the media and run the government, that's right on their doorstep. I think Irvine Welsh has broken out of that now but the Scots are patronised by the English press, dismissed as 'Scottish writers' now when they're bigger than that. Alan Warner's coming out of it with his last book, *The Sopranos*, and that's because he's such a good writer but it's always in the media's mind to do it. It's like them saying *The Football Factory* is a 'football book' and John King is a 'football writer'. It's their way of putting you over to the side – 'he's like Richard Allen who writes *Skinhead*'. Fuck off! I think the sad side of this new literature is that on the back of *Trainspotting* suddenly there's all these books about drugs, all these things that are set in Camden Town written by graduates. Publishers have tried to get in on it but they don't understand what's really going on. When people pick up a book they're looking for more than just a transparent 'I took lots of whizz' story. You can actually see this with the way the covers are now. Go into the original paperback section and there's all these covers of *Ecstasy* and *The Football Factory* – there's all those bright colours. They've just followed on that sharp Jonathan Cape design. I think there's still a snobbery in publishing. They're saying 'OK we can do some young writers'. Maybe we are young compared to other writers but I mean I think it's really the writing that is different. The eighties were empty. What was in the seventies? You probably have to go back to Alan Sillitoe and people like that for writing which was actually looking at things from a different point of view, in England, and I'm talking about England not Britain. In the seventies you just had Richard Allen. He sold two million copies of *Skinhead* and that was because there was nothing else, people were desperate.

**S. R.** Why is your writing so graphic, in-your-face and realistic?

**J. K.** I think it's just making a decision to be honest. I think it really is about being honest and saying do you want to write something that's real and accurate and is true or do you want everyone to think 'oh isn't he a nice person and isn't he right on'. And you have to make that decision. I think there's an awful lot of writers who are just obsessed with being a 'writer', having people call them an 'author' – it's the difference between wanting to be a writer and wanting to write. These authors want everyone to think isn't he a nice person and he's got all the right views and everything. You can still have a good view, and present things honestly whether you're talking about football, sex, politics, whatever. So I think it's just making that decision.

It's hard to say about influences because it's like you're copying someone so I think you can only say the things that you like. Alan Bleasdale's *Boys From The Blackstuff* for me was one TV series in the eighties. Shakehands was going round and he was going over to this table and the blokes who were sitting there had wedges and they had like pink jumpers on and it was just so right and I'd never seen that on the screen. I thought that's just like it is down the pub or at football on a Saturday. It was just so right, real. I can remember seeing *Scum* when it came out. To me, the two worst things I've seen in the cinema were the rape of the boy in *Scum* and *Last Exit To Brooklyn* where there was a gang-bang, rape, whatever you want to call it. Those are two times in the cinema when I felt really sickened. But think how strong *Scum* was – that was Alan Clarke more than twenty years ago. Carlin was a hero, a real character.

I think in the seventies films were a lot tougher. It was much more hard-hitting the things that they were putting out. I don't think my writing is that brutal. To me there's always a hope there. It's the same with Irvine's writing. The characters aren't really victims. They have strength and pride. In Irvine's case he's writing about Scotland and Leith and what's happened there when the train doesn't run anymore but if you look at his characters there's a positive feeling and humour. The character getting out and making the money or changing from heroin to Ecstasy, for that area it's a big positive thing, anti-heroin.

I think with *The Football Factory* it's a bit different, there's a different politics in the South, even though the people are basically the same. A lot of the white working- and lower middle-class voted for Thatcher. There is a difference and there is a similarity. There's a lot more opportunities down here. In my book the characters are all working. They're not on the eighty-eighth floor and wearing flat caps. I think my books are positive. Tommy Johnson uses racist language but he has black mates. He talks sexist with his friends but respects women and hates 'nonces'. He is actually a moral man. I believe all of my books are moral books, but on an everyday level. The establishment thinks it holds the copyright on morality but it doesn't.

**S. R.**  What about football? Do you still go to football?

**J. K.**  I went to my first game in 1970. The first time I went to every home game was 1976. I stood in the Shed. It's changed. It's changed and it hasn't changed, that's the funny thing. Like in Stockholm [for Chelsea's 1998 European Cup Winner's Cup Final win] there were twenty-five thousand men there between the age of twenty-five and forty-five. There were blokes there who were our heroes, six or seven years older than us, 'leaders' of the Shed, staying in the Sheraton Hotel. And a lot of these blokes have made money. They're no mugs, even though they might look back on it with a little bit of embarrassment they'll probably say they were the best days of their life. So yeah, I think it's changed. I think, you know, like in the eighties the aggro was all played up, by Thatcher and the press. I think it was all played up too much. I mean OK there was a big young population going around and there was a lot of trouble but if you're at a riot like Chelsea versus Sunderland in 1985 – OK there was trouble there but not as much as they made out. There was more trouble up at Sunderland that was never reported, in the back streets, but that was always the case. For me it's interesting the way the media behaves – why is football-related violence such a big thing? And it's to do with the media. Things were going on in the twenties and thirties that were far worse than happens now. One of my Dad's mate's father-in-law – he's dead now – lived in Poplar. I can remember in the eighties one Christmas he's sitting there, 'youngsters today – they're nothing special' and he started going into this big thing about how they used to go with West Ham down to Millwall – they were called the Ironworkers, this is the twenties and thirties, and he was big in the unions. And he said they'd go down in the mornings, said there'd be running battles all day, said that all the street lamps would be smashed, that there'd be stabbings and that, inside the ground, bottle fights, and it would go on till late at night.

The difference now from the eighties was that then it was over-reported. And now it's under-reported. And if you look at who is reporting it, it's certain papers controlled by certain people so now they want to make football nice and glossy and start targeting middle-class people who were never interested in football before. Another myth is that no middle-class people or women ever went to football in the old days. Again, that's rubbish. You know you still get big punch-ups in London between say Chelsea and Tottenham or Chelsea and West Ham at the end of last season. But that never gets in the papers because it's away from the ground and the only things you actually see are inside the ground. We're a society led by TV news and for that you need film footage. Like Marseille, where basically you've got two hundred drunk youths throwing bottles that never hit anybody and tear gas floating over the yachts. They never report an Englishman getting his throat cut down a back alley; people who were there at France '98 would say that the local Arab population were going round robbing them and cutting them up. There's a book called *Football Hooligans: Knowing the Score* by Gary Armstrong which is very interesting. He has some good ideas on hierarchies, the media and space.

**S. R.**  Why do you think your fiction has captured the changes in male football culture better than most academic studies? Is it because of your own observations as a fan?

**J. K.**  Because you're writing through the character and you've got a lot more freedom. You get some factual books that are written and half the time they don't know whether to condemn it or love it. That is a problem within people. If you were to talk to most people who are involved today, few of them would say it's right. One of the important things about writing is being honest, it's sort of saying what's the relationship between Chelsea and West Ham through the years; or Chelsea and Millwall. Obviously you have to know to begin with, and a lot of people are busking it, relying on newspaper stories. The papers don't have a clue. A good number of Chelsea fans come from the shires, from the new towns. You get a different sort of thing from

West Ham and Millwall. But then West Ham and Millwall have changed now because of the gentrification of London and the increase in prices of property. What happened over in West London and South London and places like Stevenage before is now going out to Essex, and going down towards Margate and places like that. That's quite an interesting thing. It's difficult. It's not like the old days. But then having said that, it could be age.

We have had some great football under Gullit and Vialli. They say Chelsea has got all these new people coming but you don't really see them. If you go in the East Stand in the forty pound seats you'll see them but I don't go there. In the pubs I go in, it's just blokes who have gone for a long time or younger lads who are the same as you. I don't go away as much now to be honest with you. I mean in the eighties we used to go from Slough. We used to take one or two coaches, between fifty and a hundred blokes. It was a lot easier. I think people stopped going because of the expense. You can't get tickets unless you're a season ticket holder. Plus clubs give you between eighteen hundred and two thousand tickets. So you haven't got that same freedom you used to have. When we were in the Second Division we would take between six and ten thousand to away games. Because you could get the tickets easily or turn up on the day more people went. I go to some but I don't go to as many as I used to. Because otherwise you're spending a hundred pounds. I can afford it now but three years ago I couldn't. I think what's sad is the singing. There's no songs anymore. Chelsea aren't that bad. But it is different to how it was. They say it's seats killing the atmosphere, but we were going in the seats in the eighties, in Gate 13. You had a different thing though. You had a section where the boys went and you had a couple of thousand singing. But now it's so regimented and if you're down the pub and there's ten of you three of you might have season tickets, three of you sitting over there, two of you sitting over there. It's different.

But there again like I said with Chelsea there's a lot of blokes who go in their thirties and that is still the core of the club. If I had a lot of money and I was going to invest in a club with solid support who will be back, who are in a similar position to Chelsea a few years back I would invest in Man City because they'll definitely come back.

I started supporting Chelsea on the back of the Osgood and Hudson team. After that we were shit. We'd get as many travelling away as we did at home sometimes. We went down to the old Second Division. We were terrible. But they were great days. We had a real laugh. So all this new success has come quite quickly. I think a lot of people are stretching themselves to get season tickets because they think 'we've gone twenty years and done nothing so why should we miss the pay-off'.

I used to go to England games. Yeah I went away. I think England travelling away is very lively, more so than domestic games. You get some great characters, real fun-loving people. They were some great occasions. Quite a few people used to go on their own as well because their mates didn't want to travel. I think a lot of the way a culture of a country is presented is often wishful thinking on the part of the authorities. You look at the French. The French are always pushed as being highly romantic and very cultural and very this and very that. But then if you go there – and I like France, I've been there quite a few times – but there is a seriousness, they're very straight and this is mixed in with an earthiness you find in Britain. Whereas we present ourselves – or our tourist agency presents the English gentleman – all stiff upper lip and no emotion as our representation. Then you look at mass English culture. You go into a pub and everyone's laughing and joking. You go into a bar in Europe and it's so serious. And you listen to the news. OK there are race problems in Britain. But compared to somewhere like Germany or France or Italy it just doesn't compare. You look at punk, you went to a punk gig and it was just reggae, solid reggae. Look at the music today – techno, jungle, drum and bass. If you look at football as well. All the London mobs at one time or other since the 1970s have either been led by or have had one of the top lads who is black. I tend to look at the English culture, British culture, and it is very lively. And it's probably not as violent as a lot of other cultures. You think what is the media all about. I've had that when I've gone to Italy or France – 'English fans are all Nazis'. That's not true; the National Front gets thirty per cent of the vote in France. We don't get any elected, they don't even get their deposit back if they stand. You've got the right on law and order and you've got the trendy left who will never say it hates the 'common people' but it does, so it has to find a nice way of saying it so it says they must all be right-wing so you've got those two sides. It's always the outsider. In *The Football Factory* I try to show that the main character isn't an outsider, that the things that are important to him are things that are in the culture. The main difference is that his language is more up front and he takes the violence to a logical conclusion.

**S. R.** What are you writing now and what do you expect your future writing to be?

**J. K.** I'm just finishing a novel called *Human Punk*. The character will be a bit different to those in my previous books, which were about showing the potential in some of those people who were considered bogeymen by the establishment, the mythical thug roaming the streets with a shaved head tipping over prams. *Human Punk* will be set in the new town Slough, and the character is heavily influenced by punk, someone who does his own thing, on his own terms. It's set in three time zones, and shows how punk has influenced our culture, the DIY attitude we've been talking about. At the same time the book will be looking at the satellite towns around London, the land outside the M25 boundary, how people are marginalised and dismissed as having no culture.

I've got a stack of short stories and have had a few published in anthologies – 'Last Train Home' in Stewart Home's *Suspect Device*, 'Space Junk' in Toni Davidson's *Intoxication: An Anthology of Stimulant-Based Writing*, 'Last Rites' in Kevin Williamson's *Rovers Return* and 'The Beasts of Marseille' in Sarah Champion's *Fortune Hotel*. Two actors, Tam Dean Burn and Sal Ahmet, read 'The Beasts of Marseille' at Turnmills in Clerkenwell the other night, with visuals and music.

It was a good night. Irvine Welsh and Gary Armstrong were there, plus Martin King and Martin Knight who wrote *Hoolifan: Thirty Years of Hurt*. I did the introduction for *Hoolifan*. It's a great book, pure social history. It's important to come in from different angles. *The Football Factory* and *England Away* talked about football and society through fiction, Gary Armstrong's *Football Hooligans: Knowing the Score* in academic terms, and *Hoolifan* in a factual, historical way. 'The Beasts of Marseille' is a story of two journalists, one right-wing, the other left-wing, who misreport some England boys defending themselves in France and then go and abuse a young rent boy in their five-star hotel. The point of the story is that these journalists promote different views but are basically the same, from the same root, pontificating about things they know nothing about, dealing in generalisations, corrupt and exploitative. I want to take this on, maybe as a play and/or a short film. Nick Love is working on the screenplay for *Headhunters*. He's a top writer, and has another two screenplays on the go, *Strong Boys* and *Low Life*. British Screen has put money into the script development. *The Football Factory* is going slower, and I want to try and keep some control of this. It could easily be mucked up by people who don't understand the subject, the social and political angles stripped away. I'd rather not see it made than have rubbish come out.

The film business is slow moving. It seems to be more about money than imagination. Hopefully it will come off, it's just finding the right people. My first concern is writing and after *Human Punk* I'll be doing another novel *White Trash*. I might get *Verbal* going properly. Do it as a home-produced A5 pamphlet, same as I did the first issue. Mix all sorts of things together, not just fiction. *Two Sevens* was a good laugh, a lot of fun, I don't see why not.

**S. R.** What have you learnt from your writing work and what are the rewards?

**J. K.** I think when you're writing you don't have much confidence. Specially when it comes to 'social realism' or whatever you want to call it. You know, it's a big struggle buying the time to write, and because my three books have sold well it means I can write full-time. That's a dream come true. It means I can try to improve. The best thing about *The Football Factory* was the response of people who know the culture, whether they're men or women, old or young, and this was very positive. I got trashed by the *Guardian* and *Independent* early on but it was the reaction of ordinary people that mattered. I think I've learnt that a lot of the people who control things aren't very good at what they do. Strip away the arrogance, and they're busking it, copying what everyone else says. I think it's very important to develop what we've achieved and take it on. It's pathetic that we're approaching 2000 and our society is controlled by yes-men. What happened to pride, honesty, integrity? Suppose that's punk rock speaking.

*Gordon Legge*

# A Pop Life
Gordon Legge

*Gordon Legge was born in the early 1960s in Falkirk and was brought up in Grangemouth. He is author of* The Shoe *and* I Love Me (Who Do You Love?) *and the collections of short stories* In Between Talking About the Football *and* Near Neighbours.

*Polygon, a small but influential publishing house in Edinburgh, published his first three books which have become hard-to-find cult classics. Polygon itself suffered financial difficulties in this period but survived. James Kelman, AL Kennedy, Janice Galloway and James Meek have all been published by Polygon. Gordon Legge contributed 'Pop Life' – named after a Prince song – to* Children of Albion Rovers *and 'The Weathers and their Famous Fathers' to* Rovers Return, *both collections of novellas from Rebel Inc, and 'Moving Target' to* Intoxication. The Faber Book of Pop *edited by Jon Savage and Hanif Kureishi included an extract of his writing.*

*In 1998 he realised a lifelong ambition by filing football match reports on his beloved Falkirk for* Scotland on Sunday. *He has specialised in a kind of 'small town romance' fiction of ordinariness and obsession (with everyday passions like football and, particularly, popular music) amongst people like himself in Scotland outside the big cities of Edinburgh and Glasgow. Years before Nick Hornby's* High Fidelity *Gordon Legge was documenting in story form obsessive young (and not so young) pop and rock fandom.*

*After attending university in Edinburgh (Heriot-Watt) as a civil engineering student Legge joined Margaret Thatcher's 1980s army of young unemployed; a stint which lasted years. In the 1990s as Writer-in-Residence at the Royal Edinburgh Hospital he has edited two anthologies of writing by mental health patients. We talked in bars in Edinburgh, where Gordon Legge now lives.*

**STEVE REDHEAD** How and why did you start writing fiction?

**GORDON LEGGE** When I was unemployed for ten or eleven years, about halfway through that was when I started writing. I was quite a big reader. You tend to read when you've got a lot of time on your hands. I was a very big reader of crime fiction. Patricia Highsmith in particular I thought was good. I'd read all the Penguin modern classics and all that sort of stuff. All your French writers and Russian writers in my mid to late teens. It was crime writing that I really liked. I liked the style of particularly the American writers. I don't know if Elmore Leonard was around at that time but he's a very good example of the type of person that I liked. I liked Ed McBain as well. All these crime books were very strictly structured in terms of being like 220 pages, ten pages a chapter, 22 chapters. I wanted to do something with my life as well. My mother died in 1985 and I was about 24 then and I wanted to do something. I wasn't doing anything with my life. I was cycling roads. I was going to football occasionally. Not going to very many gigs because I didn't have much money. Buying lots of records. Lots and lots of records. Talking about records and football a lot of the time – just like the early books. One day I sort of sat down and I wanted to write a crime novel set in my environment. I'd read McIlvanney's – William McIlvanney – books. Hadn't read any James Kelman then. I quite liked McIlvanney's books. I thought they could have had reference points which I knew of – references to records, whatever. I kind of sat down one day and worked out my 22 chapters. I thought, 'oh that was fun'. And then I started writing and I thought 'oh this is really fun!' It was probably raining or something you know. I'd probably been out on my bicycle. So I just started doing it. I thought this is really, really good. I was enjoying it. It was going very quickly. It's one of the things which I've reminded myself of doing these football reports – I had to write 850 words on Saturday because one of the games was called off and I had to file 850 words worth of copy by six o'clock and I basically wrote it all after the game had finished up to quarter to six. You can write quite a lot when you put your mind to it. So the first book was quite straightforward. I bought myself a typewriter and taught myself to type. I thought this is fun as well. I really enjoyed all that stuff.

Every aspect of it was fun – the writing of it, the working on it. I was also by this time doing quite a lot of voluntary work. And I thought maybe this all ties in together. Doing the voluntary work, that kept the dole off my back. Doing the writing, that was something which might end up getting me somewhere. It's only really now, over the past six months, I'm actually sort of making money from writing. I'm still not making a lot of money. I still work as a nurse. So anyway between the typing and the actual writing I really just enjoyed everything to do with it. *The Shoe* didn't end up a crime novel. It basically became a kind of slice of life thing. I don't imagine that's the first time that's happened – or that it will be the last – that someone's attempted some genre and it hasn't come out as such.

**S. R.** How did you get published?

**G. L.** I cycled through to Polygon. I left it with them for a while. I'm a very patient person – it was about a year before they got back to me. I cycled through again and said 'hello it's me again' and they'd shifted offices and they told me it was getting published about two or three months later. And then another year passed – I wasn't very happy about that. I think I told a few people. I can't remember really. I hadn't told anybody up to this point. It's like Grangemouth where I grew up on a council estate was full of people who were writers – very druggy type stuff and all that. Delusions of grandeur maybe, if you can use that expression. I didn't want anybody to accuse me of that. So I never told anybody. But then quite a long time – seven or eight months – had passed and I hadn't heard from them, and I cycled through to see them again. They said 'oh apologies, the company's gone bust' and it was an absolutely wet day and I was thoroughly soaked and I was quite miserable probably a bit churlish and puerile. They asked if I wanted the manuscript back and I just said 'no you keep it, I'll collect it some other time when the weather's better'. I got home. A few days later my Dad came round and said some guy's been phoning up for you, trying to get in touch with you. This was Peter K who is quite important in Scottish literature. He's had to do with Janice Galloway, James Kelman and all that. Peter was editor who was taking over at Polygon and he said 'Look we're going to publish the book, everything's OK'. The rest is kind of history as regards that. It was a long time. I do have loads of patience. I must have had loads of patience back then. I never pressurised them or anything.

**S. R.** What about your influences? Who and what were they?

**G. L.** By the time I had the first book out I was aware of James Kelman and I noted that he alternated between novels and short story collections, and still does. I thought, I suppose, I could work on a book of short stories. I started writing them. Again that was incredible fun because the first book of short stories it was like I would sit down and write stuff and about forty five minutes later I would say 'oh that's that'. This procedure has all changed. Now I am painstakingly slow and all that sort of stuff. But then it would be like I would write something and forty five minutes later I would say 'that'll do, it's a good story'. I was a big admirer by this time of Raymond Carver as well – and in the first book too – and American short story writers who followed that, Alice Munro (she's Canadian) as well. I just loved anything to do with the short story. I was amazed that so many things kept coming into my mind – 'I must have wrote that before? No I haven't'. Everything just seemed as if I had this whole world to myself, writing about people who were on the dole who were pretty obsessed about records and football. It was quite an easy thing to do in some respects.

**S. R.** Why did you write about the subject matter you did?

**G. L.** Nobody was really writing that then. It's a thing I always say when I turn up at writers' groups to do workshops – which is a thing I don't do very often, I don't really enjoy it – that the great thing is to be original, and they all look up at you and smile at you and say 'I'm original' and they'll show you their ghost story. I was just very fortunate in what I was doing. There really was a touch of originality in there. Duncan McLean was the first writer I befriended. Basically through *Clocktower Press*. Duncan also knew the people at Polygon. His first book was originally supposed to come out with Polygon but it didn't. It was poached by the people down South! But it was interesting meeting Duncan. He knows his music. He knows a bit about football. It's one of the things which always happens to my writing world which is different to my other world. Have you seen that film *My Name is*

*Joe?* You know there's the bit where they're talking to each other across the table – him and the woman – and he's saying 'White Man At Hammersmith Palais' and she's saying The Clash. They're going like that through the records. That doesn't happen in real life. Where it does happen is with the people I've met through the book world. They say like 'What was the B-side of Ambition?' and everybody knows. This is serious trainspotter, anal stuff. Paul Reekie, when Damon from Blur was up, Damon had got ATV confused with The Television Personalities, and Paul Reekie didn't want anything to do with Damon from Blur because imagine making a mistake as stupid as that! And all these people – Alan Warner, Irvine Welsh, Paul Reekie, Duncan McLean – they all have incredibly good knowledges of music. And I just thought it was me and a few pals from Grangemouth that sort of knew about reggae and knew about soul and knew about the Velvet Underground. And you meet Alan Warner who was such a Can obsessive that he travelled over to Germany. You meet Irvine Welsh who once got in a fight with Geoff Dean who used to play with Modern Romance or Blue Rondo A La Turk or one of those kind of groups. That's where it becomes really great and all that. There's the bonding of football as well. Everybody was quite obsessive – I hate the word obsessive from my mental health work, though I use the word. Everybody knew their stuff when it comes to music.

I think it was Simon Frith that told me this, that when he was working with *Melody Maker* the editor's idea of the ideal very loyal reader was somebody (male) who stayed in a town just outside Middlesbrough who didn't have a girlfriend. This was what they looked forward to every single week, this was the highlight of their week – reading *Melody Maker* or *NME*. Most of the provinces, and the towns that surround the provinces, things like music they take a hold. Punk was still strong for a long time up here. Acid house was still very strong up here. The Scottish hardcore scene, the happy hardcore scene, it is basically to acid house what 'oi' was to punk – it's that kind of boom boom boom all the time. It's just taking the basic elements. Things like that do stick longer in the provinces. We rely more on this. We don't have the same input from friends and all that to change us. My friends who I talk with about records are very good but there's not an awful lot. It's not a matter of somebody saying 'Have you heard this great new record?' and all that sort of stuff. That doesn't happen all the time. It happens with my good friends fairly regularly but then again I'm getting the same sources as they are – through the radio, through the papers, whatever. It's not a case of people I know going to clubs and saying 'I heard this great tune at a club blah blah blah'. Again the money thing came into it. You didn't have the money to go out and see too many bands. You can also tie that in to a love of the journalists from the music press at that time. The stalwarts – the Nick Kents, the Charlie Shaar Murrays, the people who came in with punk, particularly Tony Parsons, Julie Burchill and Paul Morley – a 'Manchester' man, still a big hero of mine. He could have done anything. I once sent stuff off to *NME* where I reviewed a couple of records. It didn't get printed. It was probably rubbish. That was just after my mother died.

Interesting thing that's come about with the football. Three or four really good friends – all we talk about is records and football. I've been saying that probably records are my number one hobby – it's the same with my friends – but football is great to talk about and it's great to write about (like I've been doing the last couple of weeks). I love being a fan of pop music, I love going out and buying records. As soon as I realised your train was late I was straight off to the record shop – I spent about £20 on records (an illegal version of the Stardust single 'Music Sounds Better With You' which has the original Madonna sample and two or three dance compilations which they were flogging off cheap). But I didn't really want to write about pop music. I wanted to write about the people I grew up with. And also we were quite politicised towards the end of the late eighties, in the wake of the miners' strike and Mrs Thatcher and all that kind of stuff. I didn't see writing a book as an inroad into writing for a music paper. I do elevate these people to gods as well you know! Steven-Seething-Wells, I disagree with 99% of what he says but I think he's a great writer. A friend of a friend of a friend is Keith Cameron who is now one of the big writers with *NME* and I still elevate him to god status. I'm not too sure I could write about pop music. I'm not too sure I could review gigs and albums and all that.

I never thought I could do football games. I wrote an article on Prince for a newspaper earlier this year – it's a Scottish writing thing, there are certain acts that we all like. Prince is one of them, he's not the trendiest person in the world anymore. Prince is one of those ones that people get surprised – people say 'Oh I like Prince' 'cos the papers don't like him anymore but we still do. I think it's a provinces thing again.

**S. R.** How did fanzines influence you?

**G. L.** I do revere things like *NME*, and *Mojo* and *Cut* – these things are just for my generation as well. You look through *Mojo* and whatever and think how can people who are younger than me possibly understand all this, all these references to Bob Dylan and jokes about the man who shouted 'Judas'. It was the 'Free Trade Hall' not the 'Royal Albert Hall'. Anyone who is coming to that for the first time – I daresay they can take it all in – but it does look like it's an in-joke. The letters pages as well. The style magazines as well – they're from my generation. I was reading fanzines at that time, whenever I came through to Edinburgh or Glasgow I would pick up fanzines. Mainly music. I don't know which football ones were around in the mid-eighties. *The Absolute Game* is now edited by Paul Hutton, who I go to the Falkirk games with, it's a small small world. I certainly saw *The Absolute Game* in its infancy. *Not The View* I used to get that. I thought that was tremendously funny. I can't remember when the first Falkirk one started. I was aware of it. I wouldn't have said it was a big influence. But the music fanzines were. I think, as well, the fanzine writing wasn't as good as the music press. It was maybe more enthusiastic. Many of the fanzine editors quickly moved on to the music press or the football press. You've actually floored me! I did used to read fanzines a lot. I'm sure if I went back through the piles of paper I'd be astonished at the number that are there. I did read them fairly religiously. At that time anything that mentioned a group I liked I would read it. I don't bother so much these days with fanzines. I get the Falkirk fanzine when it comes out. They usually just look at each other, moan at the board or whatever. The humour does seem to have gone out of the fanzines now. It used to always be humour. I saw *The End* fairly early on. I liked that 'cos that did seem to be about the humour, the ritual of going to the game and all that. Up here now it just seems to be a certain moaning about the board all the time. And things like to do with the ground. We have a standing ground and we're probably going to have to ground share. It's not looking very good for us in that respect. It was better when it was anagrams and all that, ins and outs, you can't go wrong with that.

**S. R.** What made you stay with the Scottish fiction scene, Polygon and Edinburgh and so on?

**G. L.** I think it was part of my contract to do another book with them. I can't remember whether I took time off from writing. I'd worked this out – novel, short stories, novel, short stories. When you finish one you don't want to write another novel. When you've done a book of short stories, you're sick of the sight of short stories. It does seem to work that way. *I Love Me*? I think I was still staying in Grangemouth when I started writing it. I moved to Edinburgh in 1992. I'm terrible with dates. Basically I got the job as writer-in-residence at the pyschiatric hospital (Royal Edinburgh). Part of my voluntary work at Falkirk entailed working in a pyschiatric hospital. There was an advert came up for a writer-in-residence at the Royal Edinburgh Hospital. They wanted someone with pyschiatric experience who was up for writing. I fitted the bill perfectly and luckily got the job. So I moved to Edinburgh and around that time *Rebel Inc* was just starting up. I think I moved to Edinburgh two or three months later. Kevin Williamson got in touch with me. So it was very good for me, for my social life. Irvine Welsh did a reading at the first *Rebel Inc* thing I think. I think I had two books out before Duncan McLean's first book. Duncan was very much involved in this group. I think the first couple of *Clocktower Press* booklets came out before *Rebel Inc*. And none of us come from Edinburgh. Alan Warner is from Oban, Kevin Williamson is from Thurso, Duncan McLean is from a wee town just outside Aberdeen. I'm from Grangemouth. Irvine Welsh is from Leith – we would not call that Edinburgh. An accident of geography I think! It helped being in Edinburgh. I wrote the first two books without really knowing anybody. Then when it came to meeting people it was a relief to hear people having the same problems. You'd quiz them for their approaches – did they suffer the same sort of disillusionment, or the same reactions when things went wrong, or right? That was quite good. But meeting these people. The good thing was the bonding. We didn't really talk about books – if we would we would all have read the same books. We'd all read *The Diceman*, we'd all read *Nausea*, we'd all read Richard Brautigan. I was astonished to discover that other people had read Richard Brautigan. I couldn't believe it. I thought that was a Grangemouth thing. Again, other people liked Patricia Highsmith. I remember when I first heard of Patricia Highsmith. It was not in a fanzine but in a music magazine called *Jamming*. Mark Perry used to do a column in there about good books. He was talking about James Joyce and Patricia Highsmith. I'd read *Ulysses* which I obviously didn't do very well with. I'd read *Dubliners* which I'd really liked. He said 'Go and have a look at Patricia Highsmith'.

Meeting the other writers just the great thing was their knowledge of music. The bands they'd played in, the support gigs they'd done. Paul Reekie for instance used to play with a band called The Thursdays. But I never wanted to play music at all. I thought I could do a job for Inter Milan or AC Milan! I think with fiction there's no real editorial process. There's nobody tapping you on the shoulder. There's no collaboration, no clash of egos. There's time as well. It's hard to remember what I did – I was unemployed for ten, eleven years – how did I fill my days? I did read a hell of a lot. That's when I did the bulk of my reading. I suppose the isolation – I had a social life and family – there was an isolation there which must have lent itself to wanting to read.

**S. R.** What about other influences from popular culture – film and television for instance?

**G. L.** I don't really like films – I like *The Blues Brothers*, I like *Taxi Driver*. I went to see that *My Name Is Joe* and I thought that was poor. I've seen lots of Scottish writers being criticised for having macho characters but why didn't that film not get the same criticism? It was very much 'the characters were too goody goody'. It confused me. But film has always had that kind of aspect. I go to watch films. I went to see *The Last Days of Disco*. I thought, 'This is nonsense'. I don't really like *Reservoir Dogs*. I thought *Pulp Fiction* was quite funny. I'm not a film person. I think Irvine Welsh and Alan Warner are more into films. I used to have a couple of friends that I did employment training scheme with, who'd be up on a Friday afternoon. We'd go and watch the new release at the pictures 'cos it was only a pound to get in. Especially the ritual of going I quite liked. Now it's the ritual of going along with my girlfriend. I like all the things that surround it but the actual content of films, no. If you think that there's someone on the other side of the camera saying 'that'll look great, that'll look great, that'll look just wonderful!'. And you know that things have been adapted, that everybody's acting and that they all get paid huge amounts of money and they're all very middle-class. And everybody involved in it is middle-class.

TV would be an influence on me, that can't be denied. I grew up with what people would say was the golden age of television. Again I thought a lot of it was rubbish. *Boys From The Blackstuff* I really liked. I couldn't handle most of the repeats of it funnily enough. I just saw flaws in it. I can't remember if I was writing by that time or not. You do have a different approach to things when you're doing it yourself. You do notice the repetitions that appear within the dialogue, inappropriate repetitions. Repetitions can be used effectively in some circumstances.

**S. R.** This is a very male world – the writers and the subject matter – rather like people said the 'Beat Generation' was. Why do you think that is?

**G. L.** I read William Burroughs and Jack Kerouac. I liked Burroughs' later books – I thought they were really good reads. Very well written. Easy to read. *Junkie* and *Naked Lunch* I didn't enjoy as much. I found them hard work. I liked the later stuff, the big chunky ones, they were almost potboilers. As for Kerouac I read two or three of his books. I've never finished *On The Road*. I've tried it again every two or three years but I don't enjoy it. It does nothing for me I must admit. I'm not aware of Ginsberg at all. You can maybe put Richard Brautigan in with that. Some people would say he was the last of the 'beats' or the first of the 'hippies'. Brautigan's stuff I loved. It just tickled me. I don't know why. He just amazes me. I cry! I've tried to start conversations on these lines with Alison Kennedy and Janice Galloway who are very nice and very clever, incredibly clever – far more clever than I am. I've also talked with various girlfriends over the years when they came in and see a house covered in records and CDs and I'm going on about going to the football and all that and talking about football all the time and they look at you as if you're daft. I genuinely think it's the wrong way round. I think women should be getting into these things. To go through life without interests, hobbies, call it what you like, is wrong. My girlfriend just now she looks at the CDs and records and I tell her how much I spend, £40 or £50 a week, and she just thinks that's completely loony. I say 'Well what do you do? What are your interests?' And she says 'Well I like music'. But she doesn't buy papers or magazines. I don't know why it is. Women traditionally spent money going shopping. If you go to charity shops there's always more female clothes in there than male clothes. In charity shops it's really noticeable. One rack of male clothes and four or five racks of female clothes.

I have been to gigs all my life. I still go to lots of gigs. I go with Neil Cooper who is music critic at *Scotland on Sunday* and we always sit and reminisce about the first few gigs we went to and they were exclusively male. They were very much this idea of a *Melody Maker/ NME* type reader. Nowadays you go to gigs and at least a third of the audience is female. And they're not there being dragged along as 'girlfriends', they're there because they want to be there. There are women coming to football, more women interested, but it's still a tiny tiny minority. Football is not something you just turn up to. You have to go all the time to appreciate it, to get into it. I find there are more female readers in the country. I don't get much fan mail nowadays but the first couple of books I got a lot of fan mail, most of which was female, people who liked listening to John Peel and that. Still when I turn up at writers' groups I'm astonished when women of all generations come round and say I really liked that, young women, women in their sixties and seventies.

**S. R.** Why in the end did you leave Polygon?

**G. L.** I remember when *Trainspotting* first came out, I thought it was going to be huge. Two or three others did. I don't think Irvine thought it would be huge. I don't think even his publishers thought it would be huge. I got a letter from Robin Robertson when I was still working as writer in residence at the hospital saying 'I have always admired your stuff, get in touch sometime'. Basically I didn't get back to them for a long time. I didn't really want to leave Polygon. They'd done good books and they were friends of mine. I went in to see them and had loads of cups of tea and told them all my problems. It was just two girls, very friendly. But the money thing had to be considered. Also I was contractually obliged to stay with Polygon. I had a heart to heart with Marion who ran Polygon. She was quite happy. So basically she said I could go and talk to Jonathan Cape. Me and Robin Robertson met and discussed the short stories and he wanted some taken out and some changed. I said 'It's OK, you can change a couple but I ain't changing other ones'. He's OK. I think the financial thing comes into it. Warner's done very well for them. Irvine's done very well. There's a trickle down effect. There was a good chance I could have done well for them. I didn't! I think it's sold fairly well. I think they're slightly disappointed but I'm still selling better than other Cape ones. I haven't done any creative writing for seven or eight months. I started writing a rock and roll novel but I didn't finish.

Emer Martin

# **Dubliner**
Emer Martin

*Born in the late 1960s, Emer Martin is from Dublin. She is author of
two novels,* Breakfast in Babylon *and* More Bread Or I'll Appear. *She
provided 'Teeth Shall Be Provided' for Rebel Inc's* Rovers Return *and is
a contributor to the Irish fiction anthology* Shenanigans *and the travel
fiction collection* Fortune Hotel.

Breakfast In Babylon *won Ireland's Book Of The Year Award for
1996 at the prestigious Listowel Writers' Week. The novel was first
published in 1995 by Wolfhound in Dublin, and then in 1997 by
Houghton Mifflin in the USA where it was – bizarrely – described
as the 'female* Trainspotting*'! Isolt, the main female character in the
book, has been seen by Mia Dinelly – interviewing Emer Martin for*
Female FYI *magazine – as someone who makes 'Thelma and Louise
look like two old aunts from the Waltons'. Emer Martin argues that she
was writing about real people and real events in this debut novel and
that the book is a composite of fact and fiction.* Breakfast in Babylon
*may be filmed in the near future. Her second novel* More Bread Or I'll
Appear, *published in the USA in 1998, was eagerly awaited.*

*Emer Martin strongly argues that 'all smart, hip women' are feminists
and that women should not pay attention to 'the rotten mainstream culture
that tells you what you should look like, who you should sleep with and
what you will become'.* More Bread Or I'll Appear *was spotted by
fans and potential publishers – in the form of a couple of chapters –
on an 'Irish girls in New York' website for her performance group, Irish
Women Artists and Performers Collective which goes under the banner
'Banshee'.*

*Apart from Dublin in Ireland, Emer Martin has lived in various places
including London, Amsterdam, Paris, San Francisco and Savannah as
well as Israel. She now lives in New York. We conversed by e-mail
over several weeks.*

**STEVE REDHEAD** Why and how did you first start writing fiction?'

**EMER MARTIN** I wrote my first poem when I was 9 years old and drew a picture for it. It was about a disruptive horse that played golf with a rubber band. I went around the school yard reading it to anyone who would listen and the reaction was so positive that I decided to pursue it further. Every night I would write a poem and draw a picture. I had loads of these notebooks in plastic bags in my wardrobe. Due to my addiction to novels I failed every exam in school but had ploughed through the classics and at fourteen discovered William Burroughs' *Cities of the Red Night*, which was a revelation and very disturbing. I fled Ireland when I was seventeen and thought I would go and live in noble exile like Joyce, Wilde, Beckett, Shaw etc. Instead I ended up packing shelves in Safeway on the Walworth Road.

The first place I lived outside Ireland was Paris. The eighties were pretty dull everywhere, there was nothing going on in London and Dublin, everyone I knew was depressed and on the dole. Paris had a big scene. I spent my days on the slope of the Centre Georges Pompidou with a bunch of freaks. There was a whole scene going on there. Acrobats, Africans standing on boxes pontificating, Arab hustlers, mad Iranian exiles and every black sheep from every corner of Europe seemed to gather there for no good. I was sleeping in friends' apartments or in parks and spending the days hustling, begging, the odd baby sitting job etc. I wrote all the time. I kept my notebooks with me and as soon as I filled them up I threw them away. I never felt the need to keep any of these frantic scribblings. To be honest I couldn't be arsed to carry them around with me. All I had was a backpack full of poetry collections, lots of make up and a few bits of clothes, and a camera. I travelled for years, Africa, the Middle East, all over Europe. But I always came back to Paris. There was a five year period in my life when I knew I could just bunk a train to Paris and walk up to the St Michele fountain and that night be in a squat. Through all this I was writing fiction, poetry, long rants etc. and throwing them away. It was the act itself which I was focused on. Not the result. Like everyone who strums a guitar does not do it to get a recording contract. I drifted over to America and spent a year waitressing and exploring. I remember being in Mexico on my own and filling a whole exercise book with words. I threw it away in Cuba.

Eventually I settled in New York and felt the urge to write something and keep it. I was ready for *Breakfast in Babylon* when it came time to write it because I had put so much groundwork in over the years. I was used to processing my thoughts into words and getting them on paper. I don't think I would have been able to write such a work if it were not for all the practice I had gotten. The first thing I wanted to write about was the mad Paris scene in the eighties. It has disappeared now. I go back and the slope is empty. I guess other cities picked up and the scene moved on. The whole rave scene came at the end of that. Many people who contact me contact me because they remember that scene and were part of it. They are amazed to find it documented. I suppose that's a good part of fiction. History gallops by and people like us who were not the leaders or the wealthy get lost. We disappear. Only in fiction can a place be assigned to our stories. Fiction is like a microscope for our marginalised lives. Most of the people I knew ended up pretty badly. Heroin and prison and one got burnt to death in a squat fire. So I can't say there was a happy ending. I could always see it coming. As Isolt said in *Babylon* when Becky died 'God bless your eyesight – when you saw the flames from far away you woke us all to warn us. But as we fled for shelter in the coming years, you had stood, as if trapped in some childhood dream, unable to move.'

I write fiction now to get published. All of the short stories and the novella were commissioned. I knew when I was writing my second novel *More Bread Or I'll Appear* that it would be published. Even when I was writing *Breakfast in Babylon* I was so naive about the publishing industry that I never once doubted that it would be a book in print in shops. And so it was. So writing fiction has changed for me in that way, but I still write out of the same need. Maybe to disengage me from obsession, or my desire to record the silent, to trace the invisible, to reinstate the vanished. Who the fuck knows? I write about characters that are on the fringes, often through gender, race or class. Or all three. My stuff to some extent is about people who are trying to find a life worth living beyond the system. Maybe I write fiction and read others' fiction to redress the balance. It can't ever do that but it is something.

Life to me is painful and often intolerable. I don't have a God or religion so the only bit of transcendence I get is through art. When I go to the Met and look at the paintings and weird sculptures or when I read a great book or listen to some cool music, it renews my faith in humanity for a brief moment. At least till I go out onto the street and meet all my fellow horrible New Yorkers. After all the wars and tearing ourselves apart throughout the centuries, the art is the only good thing left after the mess of power has been played out. It is the best of us. Fiction can't eliminate the pain but it can somehow counter it just by having it on record. Art is not a luxury to me. I have always craved books and needed them. I will always write, even though it fucks up my life, takes all my time and energy and I still can't earn enough to live on. I think that's what drives a lot of artists crazy. To produce good work you have to constantly delve into parts of yourself that most people know better to keep buried. You have to dredge up all these highly charged things. They are constantly at the surface. You spend a life doing this and never have the security of knowing if you will be able to eat and pay rent the next year. It makes for a strange existence. But it sure beats working.

**S. R.** What other literary influences do you have? What about the so-called 'chemical generation'?

**E. M.** When I was a teenager I read widely and without any pattern. I read what I could get. My older sister had all the Russian novels on her shelf and I ploughed through Tolstoy, Dostoevsky, Gogol. She had the best books, which is sad since she doesn't have time to read anymore. I loved the way the characters in Russian books always were operating in fevers and other such things. I loved the way they would have lengthy discussions on philosophy and the matters of the day. There were always lots of characters in the stories, like a huge canvas. These characters intersected at various points, massive coincidences occurred. As far as the novel went, the Russians had my attention when I was very young. Then I read all my parents' Graham Greene books. I was in the west of

Ireland when I was thirteen on one of those Government Re-education Camps they call the Gaeltacht, sneaking out of Irish singing classes and horrible dances to read *The Power and the Glory*. It was a paperback and I had it squashed in my coat pocket. The whiskey priest was a figure that stuck with me. In my last novel *More Bread Or I'll Appear* I end with the whiskey priest, though he's not executed, rather his face is wrapped in bandages from a plastic surgery operation. I read two books a week, I went into bookshops and browsed and picked up stuff that looked interesting. I discovered Knut Hamson's *Hunger* like this and Doris Lessing and Kathy Acker and Angela Carter. Wildly diverse influences.

Poetry was a tremendous influence, both Irish and English. WB Yeats was God. He used such simple words for such complex ideas. I was stunned at how those words I used every day in language could be arranged in such a manner as to shatter all my assumptions. TS Eliot, James Joyce's *Dubliners* of course. Bernard MacLaverty was my favourite living Irish writer. He had a real sympathy for his own characters and the dilemmas of being human and fragile in viscous places. His writing is so clear and unfettered. I read everything and all books influenced me. I was lucky. I have not read too many bad books in my life. Burroughs, Kerouac, Ginsberg came when I was about fifteen years old. Then the French trooped into my life while stealing books from Shakespeare and Co in Paris: Celine, Genet, Baudelaire, Jarry, Apollinaire, Lautremont, Huysmann, Artaud. These were all my 'chemical' writers! And it wasn't always their writing that swept me away but their commitment to words. Sometimes their stuff is not the best written, it is never neat and edited, it can be unwieldy, scatological and pyschotic. But the lives they lived on the fringes, the risks they took, their drift into madness, which was reflected in their work. They were passionate artists and maniacs. I was living in parks and swallowing that myth whole. The idea of Artaud in the mental hospital during World War II, they broke his spine through repeated electric shock treatments and he kept drawing those brilliant and not so brilliant sketches. He wasn't Victor Hugo. He wasn't ever mainstream or respectable. No one would name avenues after him or put him on a coin. But he couldn't stop creating. He wasn't concerned with audience or approval or success. It was the art that moved him.

The so-called 'chemical generation' writers (I'm sure they cringe at this dubious title) – as a movement – I got wind of when I was in San Francisco for a writers' conference. I gave a reading with about ten people including Alan Warner and Kevin Williamson and ended up back at their hotel with a whole bunch of people, the writer Helena Mulkerns, my brother, my husband, a Mexican Lesbian and a few people we picked up along the way. We were diving into the pool and guzzling Glenfiddich. That was how I hooked up with that bunch of lunatics. I still have nightmares. After that Irvine Welsh came to New York and we had a savage night out with him. At one point he was being pushed through Broadway in a child's stroller we picked out of the garbage. One of us in the group took a photo. I'd love to have that photo. He was great crack, like a big mental patient let out for the day, his head was shaved and he kept hugging everyone, and shaking their bodies by gripping their heads. He even hugged and kissed my friend John Perry, a taxi driver in a seersucker suit with an empty briefcase who was leaning against the pillar in a decadent nightclub.

Warner and Williamson come over intermittently to New York to cause havoc and we hook up to talk books of course. Alan Warner's last book *Sopranos* was wonderful. I just finished reading Irvine Welsh's recent book *Filth* that lived up to its title. He got terrible reviews in America in places like the *New York Times Book Review*, which is always a good sign. I'm not sure that the American literary establishment is ready for a writer of his intensity. The depth and complexity of that book bowled me over. I want to go back now and read everything he has written. Laura Hird is also a writer that I admire and enjoy, she inspects and despises people so thoroughly. She has no mercy for her characters. These writers all have their individual styles and themes but what they have in common is a fearlessness. They write without censoring themselves or pandering to any notion of what and who is worth writing about.

**S. R.** What popular cultural influences are there on your writing?

**E. M.** Unpopular influences! The Greeks, The Bible and WB Yeats certainly. Popular mmm? In *Breakfast in Babylon* music was a big part of the character Christopher's life. He had grown up in Detroit and hit adulthood in the early seventies, a hey day for Detroit sounds. He was obsessed with Motown, MC5, The Stooges etc. Especially Iggy Pop. Like every junkie he believes that everything in life has a parallel in an Iggy Pop song, you just have to look for it. Iggy Pop was no ordinary performer. He was a poet. His song lyrics are unlike anyone else's. Depth and sorrow and hilarity in one line. I think that's why writers respond to him. When Christopher is at his lowest point in the book he sings: 'There's nothing in my dreams but some ugly memories/Kiss me like the ocean breeze'. Isolt, the other main character, listens to Velvet Underground at one pivotal moment: 'I am a lazy son/I never get things done/But here comes the ocean/Here comes the sea'. Actually, maybe it is just the ocean that is influencing me. So *Breakfast in Babylon* is set in the late eighties among people who live on the street, don't have TVs; the music is rock music from the seventies.

   *More Bread Or I'll Appear* deals with a different set of individuals. A family constantly in front of the TV. The first line is 'Where I grew up there was a trinity evident from birth: television history and the church; death as entertainment, death as catalyst, death as salvation'. Popular culture is immediately on a par with the past and God. Throughout the book the characters watch *ER* and *Seinfeld* and in the American section life begins to imitate talk shows. Orla the sister gives her son up for adoption and regrets it and goes to try and get him back when he is fifteen and ill. She sees things in terms of talk shows. 'There will be no TV audience forgiveness', she says to herself at one point, as if that is ultimately the great Greek Chorus of our society, that Oprah/Jerry Springer audience booing our infidelities. That would be the great popular influences in *More Bread Or I'll Appear*. The talk shows that addict all us foreigners when we first arrive in the United States and then become so ordinary we never tune in again.

**S. R.**  What influence has feminism had on your writing?

**E. M.**  My mother and father, Marguerite and Eamonn, were feminists. In golf clubs and tennis clubs in Ireland, women could not be full members and my parents thought that was disgusting so they started an organisation and they changed things. Directly because of them Ireland is a different place. That impressed me. I have a tendency to be cynical and lethargic when it comes to politics but that convinced me that being an activist actually does get things done. That was always the thing in our house, watching TV, the news, political programmes, my mother would ask 'Where's the woman? Spot the woman.' Nothing has changed. I still watch all the UN and NATO crap and talk and treaties and think 'Where's the woman? Spot the woman.' Sometimes there are women sitting there at the negotiating table but they're usually interpreters. Many people think that feminism has done its job and that women have equality and they take the new freedoms for granted. This is dangerous; we must keep pushing and moving forward, because things can easily go backwards. Look at the Muslim world. Islamic fundamentalism has shoved women back into a mediaeval way for life. Things can get worse so women have to keep the struggle going. I'm still waiting for the revolution. When I look at the Irish Writers Posters, it's all men. Where are the female Joyces and Wildes and Becketts? I hate those posters. Something for the tourists, but to me it is so glaringly obvious that there are dirty dealings at work when fifty per cent of your population is silenced. To counter the fact that only men's voices seemed to be acceptable we founded a group in New York for Irish women artists called 'Banshee'. We perform as a collective all over downtown New York and have a website – banshee.cnhost.com. My parents came to one of the shows when they were visiting New York and afterwards my mother said, 'not one of you has a shy bone in your bodies'. She said her generation would have never got up and behaved like we did, but that her generation laid the ground for us so that we can be outrageous, obscene and have the confidence in our work that we all have. I grew up confused. I wanted to do things with my life but the only women they ever talked about, as role models, were Joan of Arc, Florence Nightingale and Mother Teresa. Joan of Arc was some schizophrenic who listened to the voices in her head and got burnt at the stake, Florence Nightingale ran around in a strange bonnet wielding a lamp trying to mop up the mess after the men waged war, and Mother Teresa was a right-wing

Catholic who didn't believe in birth control or abortion in a country where the population rises every year by twelve million. When we had to take a saint's name for confirmation I picked Joan; at least she got to kill people!

People aren't trained to trust women, they don't even trust women bus drivers and this extends to art as well. Many men have told me to my face that they just don't read women writers. When I brought out *Breakfast in Babylon* people were shocked that a woman would write like I do. There was a passage where Isolt gets her period and has no money for tampons so she has to wrap toilet paper around her knickers and go out and sit on the street and beg. Jesus, did people complain. It was only one passage but they wanted to know why I should write such a thing. What woman hasn't done that at some point in her life? Men have been writing graphically for centuries but women's bodies are still taboo. In *Breakfast in Babylon* Isolt speaks of her frustration as a woman: 'It's like going mad. Everything you read, everything you see on TV, all the films, all the conversations you take part in. You want to talk about it all the time and it starts to get on people's nerves. You hate the culture that spawned you and there is no escape to any other system that will improve your status. If I was black I might go to Africa, somewhere where I would never see a white person again. As women we have to live in such a close proximity to those who hate us and keep us down. To finally realise the enormity of the whole rotten deal is like going mad.' Throughout the whole story she rails against the pernicious effect of religions like Christianity. At the end of the book she is standing in a church in New York 'contemplating the Pieta, grieving mother holding dead son, bereft in a mother-hating, son-killing world. The divine mercy was conditional. The God had slaughtered the Son, thirsty for life's blood and pierced the mother's heart with all the swords of sorrow he could muster. Christ running from his abusive father, absent most of his and Mary's life, Adam giving birth to Eve, the tree of life bearing poisonous fruit.' I think the world is completely off balance because of how women are treated. With so much inequality and so little justice everything is haywire. Everyone suffers when there is no equality.

**S. R.**  What about women and contemporary politics in general?

**E. M.**  As for political involvement I do nothing because I'm lazy. I was in a sex shop in LA and bought a whole bunch of stickers that said 'This Insults Women'. I thought I could stick them on advertisements and magazine covers etc. Instead I got very abstract and stuck them on random things like fire hydrants in New York. I have one on my television. 'This Insults Women'. Because I know everything will. What's wrong with us? This is a frightening time to be alive. We are in the middle of a massive extinction. Species are dying out and so too are native people and languages. We are becoming less diverse. It is all our fault. Humans are wreaking havoc on the planet and we're going to lose it without having anywhere else to go. Why the irrational behaviour? Our brains are big but not good for thought. Our brains, swollen through a trail of extinctions, have arrived in the present bloated with fantasy. We are not a logical species; we are not thinkers, we are story-tellers. As a species we are unstoppable, we are burning our forests, choking the air, mining our fields, punching a hole in the atmosphere, and yet we congratulate ourselves on being rational. The fact is that we are never persuaded by truth when prophecy will do. At nights we don't dream solutions, we absorb stories. We watch films, read books, soak up all that toxic TV.

This is what we have become after millions of minute transformations; a story-teller species. All religions have a central story that is sacred. We worship stories. They do not save us, they mesmerise us. Because we are not a rational species I don't think we'll ever sort ourselves out. We will continue to overpopulate and pollute. But since I can hold two opposing viewpoints in my head quite easily I think it is vital to keep trying to make things better and change things. Pretend there's hope. Feminism runs through all my writing. In my last book *More Bread Or I'll Appear* and its offshoot 'Teeth Shall Be Provided' the characters constantly challenge gender assumptions. Aisling, the sister who disappears, is a six foot lesbian woman 'with nipples the size of clenched fists' who likes to occasionally dress up as a man and scour the bars of Tokyo with a dildo finding gay men to fuck up the ass. If that isn't political then what is? Many people hated Aisling. My editor hated her. But she was wonderful because she was genderless, historyless, aspiritual and amoral.

I finally realised that just changing the system and demanding equal pay and childcare would never be enough for women. Society can only change when we de-emphasise gender. By gender I mean both biological sex and sexual orientation. In fact gender, race and class are the three main things in this world which affect our position in the society at large. The system has necessitated that there should be divisions in these categories that reward one side for oppressing the other. Male is to female, as straight is to gay, as white is to black, as rich is to poor. Our culture has been degraded as a result. We need an underdog to do the cheap labour. It's up to us to change this. Change never can come from the top. It's no accident that a disproportionate amount of the poor in the world are people of colour: with women at the bottom of the scale. As long as we can see the ultimate underdog as a poor dark-skinned woman then rich, white males can disassociate themselves from all guilt. Because it is so inculcated into the culture that this is the natural order of things they see no reason to alter the balance. Art should have an aesthetic end and not a moral or otherwise useful one. As Oscar Wilde said 'All Art is useless'. Though my writing is inherently political because it portrays strong women, every bit as ruthless and lusty as men, I don't sit down with an agenda. My aim is to make the language come alive and glisten and create characters so real they bleed all over the page. I will keep writing until they cut off my fingers. Then I will go home and rest.

*Mike McCormack*

# Irish Goth
## Mike McCormack

*Mike McCormack was born in Ireland in the mid-1960s. He is author of the novel* Crowe's Requiem, *published in 1997, and the short stories* Getting It in the Head.

*Getting It in the Head* won the 1995 Rooney Prize and was first published in Britain in 1996. 'The Stained Glass Violations' from that collection was also published in Shenanigans *where 'the most exciting young writers from the Irish underground' were unearthed. For the editors of* Shenanigans *'these darkly humorous tales shun Ireland's traditional topics in favour of the surreal and the deviant'. Mike McCormack's fiction epitomises these themes. It has been described as 'Irish Gothic'. In fact McCormack derives his own 'gothic' feel in his writing as much from heavy metal bands like Black Sabbath and Motorhead as Edgar Allan Poe.*

*Another successful maverick Roddy Doyle has singled out Mike McCormack's* Getting It in the Head *as 'fantastic – McCormack's stories are well written stories, very funny stories. It was almost a new place entirely that he was writing about'. For McCormack the whole 'chemical generation' label was 'bollix', especially since Irvine Welsh's* Trainspotting, *which spawned the media madness overkill, was 'that comprehensive, that good'. For McCormack the repetitive beat generation do not simply reflect 'popular culture' of the last decade – they 'are popular culture', elevating contemporary fiction to a parallel terrain with music and film in a way which has no precedent.*

*Mike McCormack now lives in the west of Ireland. While writing his second novel he took time out from that project at a busy time to complete this interview. We e-mailed each other over several weeks.*

**STEVE REDHEAD** How and why did you get into writing fiction?

**MIKE McCORMACK** I got into fiction through my reading. From my teens right through to my early twenties I was a voracious, undisciplined reader. My favourite authors during those years were Herman Hesse, Thomas Pynchon, Dostoevsky, the lesser Joyce, Flann O'Brien, John Banville and JG Ballard – a young man's reading now that I look at it. All those writers were, and still are, real heroes to me, I regarded them with the same open-mouthed awe that kids reserve now for the likes of Ryan Giggs and so on. My big discovery was Thomas Pynchon. I took a year off between secondary school and university and spent it working as a gardener in a pharmaceutical company – the best job I ever had. That was the year I did my most passionate reading. I remember getting paid and coming to Galway to buy armfuls of books and going home to read them after work. One of the books I bought was Pynchon's *V.* I was totally gobsmacked by it – the quality of the writing, the oddball characters, the combination of erudition and lunacy, most of all the sheer 'fun' of it all. His work came as such a shock to me, like 'wow, this stuff is legitimate, this is literature.' The problem with Pynchon, however, was that his work was manifestly odd and erudite. I could never hope to write anything like it. I thought he had to have dropped out of the sky or that he was from another planet.

This was the most crippling delusion I had at the time – I felt I had no credentials, no 'right' to be an author. I came from a small west of Ireland village, I was loved by my parents, I was hetero, I didn't do drugs, I drank and smoked in moderation. I had spent four uneventful years as an altar boy – a hopeless CV for any aspiring writer I thought. I went to university and spent four years there, read anything that wasn't prescribed and distinguished myself by failing English Lit. in first year and very nearly my degree. With the help of an understanding Professor I managed to scrape through by submitting only two or three essays – I found it extremely difficult to write then and it hasn't got any easier since. My philosophy Professor took pity on me and let me sign up for postgrad – I was to write a thesis on the philosophy of technology. I did loads of research, squandered a grant and a fellowship and never wrote a word of it.

About this time, however, I read Pynchon's introduction to his collection of early work, 'Slow Learner'. It is a remarkable essay, not so much for what it says, which is important in itself, but for the tone of voice in which it is cast. Pynchon sounded so recognisable, so *normal*! And I thought I recognised everything he said. The same sort of anguish about beginning to write, the same insecurities about the few things he did manage to write. I was thrilled by that essay. I reasoned that if a great writer like him suffered from these insecurities then it followed that writers had to be made not born. That reasoning I now find questionable but it served me well at the time – I started to write short stories soon after and by the time I should have submitted my thesis I had half my first book finished. I can honestly say that if I had not read that essay I would probably not have started writing in my mid-twenties – I suspect it would have been much later. Two weeks ago I met a student in Trinity College Dublin who was talking about the same essay. His feelings towards it were similar to my own. He did make the novel suggestion that it should be administered intravenously to every young writer thinking about setting out on a career in fiction. I agree.

**S. R.** What do you think of contemporary Irish fiction?

**M. M.** I've just got my copy of *Shenanigans* and I haven't read a word of it yet. What I can say about it is that it seems to be a brave venture – devoting a whole anthology to a crowd of writers most of whom have not published books before. Sarah Champion and Donal Scannell deserve real credit. It's a pity about the whole 'chemical generation' bollix which has accrued about it. It is such a cliché now, worn out after only a few years. The fact is that it was not a very fecund idea to begin with. The first book on the whole 'chemical generation' thang damn near exhausted it; *Trainspotting* was that comprehensive, that good. The drugs, the clubbing, the puking, the sex. Welsh hoovered them all up and left very little for anyone coming in his wake. Trying to put a new spin on the whole drug thing is a tall order now for those writers who concern themselves with it.

The condition of contemporary Irish fiction is as it has always been – middling. Historically the presence of a few isolated, towering geniuses – Joyce, Beckett, Flann – have obscured the fact that the greater body of Irish fiction has always been fairly mediocre. The wonder is now that without a presiding genius this should not be more obvious. At the moment there is a lot of talk about the younger generation of writers. Most of it is PR nonsense, traceable back to English editors, a myopic crowd who check in their critical faculties whenever they are confronted with an Irish manuscript. What I do find odd in the present condition of Irish fiction is the near complete absence of any experimental writing. This is doubly strange when you consider that our very best writers have all been impatient experimentalists who have gone to some trouble to expand the boundaries of fiction. You have only to think of Joyce, Beckett and Flann. Today, however, it's as if these experiments never happened, we seem to have learned nothing from them. The same goes for the more mainstream experiments like magic realism – an idiom it seems to me almost tailor-made for the Irish character. But it too might just as well never have happened. We still insist on using a jaded realism, seeing fiction as merely a mimetic device. The obsession with trying to hold a mirror up to Irish society seems to have killed off the speculative, the conjectural and the fantastical. Our writing has been the poorer for it.

**S. R.** To what extent have you and other contemporary fiction writers been reflecting the political and popular culture of the last decade?

**M. M.** There is no doubt but that these writers do reflect popular culture. What is much more interesting is the fact that they *are* popular culture also. It is now as essential to have an Alan Warner or an Irvine Welsh book as it is to have certain music or to have seen certain movies. Is this the first time contemporary fiction has had this kind of parity? This has to be a good thing – it indicates a kind of artistic and intellectual vitality beyond academia, creative writing courses or the pages of literary reviews. It's a neat idea – literature as popular culture and true to form the Americans seemed to have twigged it a long time ago. Some of the strongest writing coming out of America at the moment is being done by writers working in an unapologetically popular genre, the crime novel. James Ellroy, Ed McBain, James Lee Burke etc. are all writers who for years have been confounding the notions of literature and popular fiction as in another genre did Philip

K. Dick. Now, with the help of their readership, we have Warner and Welsh etc. doing it in newly minted genres and the helpless confusion of some commentators is almost comical. Long may it continue.

With regard to politics, the fiction of my generation seems to be marked by an apathy which would be alarming were it not for the passionless creatures which currently populate the political landscape. Let's face it, neither Blair nor Ahern present a serious threat to anyone. Neither do they inspire admiration or antipathy. With all parties trying to stake out the middle ground the resulting absence of a meaningful choice has caused fiction writers to shrug their shoulders and turn away. I wonder is this the point at which we have tried to replace politics with the type of self-consuming solipsism which characterises the 'chemical generation'.

**S. R.** What literary influences are there in your fiction?

**M. M.** All the writers I've mentioned above have influenced me in one way or another. However, the first books that left anything like a writerly impression on me were not so highbrow, they were in fact the cheap Westerns I read after I stopped reading Enid Blyton and Richmael Crompton as a child. My father had a large collection of writers like Louis L'Amour, Luke Short, JT Edson and so on. All these writers were concerned primarily with telling a story and that was good enough for me. They could also write vivid action sequences and evocative descriptive pieces. From my reading of these writers I became familiar with an image of the old West that still lives in my imagination. How that image corresponds with the historical facts is debatable but for fiction writers that is neither here nor there. In the late sixties and seventies, and on the back of all those spaghetti westerns, there developed a vogue for laconic serial heroes. They all seemed to be published by NEL and George Gilman's murderous half-breed *Edge* was definitely the high-water mark of the genre. What impressed me most at the time and what distinguished them from their relatively innocent forerunners were the descriptions of sex and the forensic detail with which knife wounds and bullet holes were described. I have a bad feeling I hoarded all this detail away.

The influence of all these Western writers did not become obvious to me until I was half way through the writing of my book of short stories. In one of the stories 'A Is For Axe' I was constructing a fight scene in a kitchen. The longer the scene went on the more obvious it became to me that I was revisiting all those bar room brawls I had read in those Westerns. Now, the more I write, the more I find myself raiding my memories of those books for techniques and devices.

As for the influence of 'literature' I think I've tried to take all the best characteristics out of all my favourite writers. When he's on form no one writes as mellifluously as John Banville. No one has his sniper's accuracy either. I learned a whole lot from him on how to write lucid, descriptive prose without befogging it with 'poetry'. Flann O'Brien is the last 'writer hero' produced in Ireland. I re-read *The Third Policeman* every couple of years just to laugh out loud. I would give a lot to have his exactness and lightness of touch. It's my favourite Irish novel, a metaphysical cartoon that always worries me. JG Ballard is the best short story writer since the war, any war you care to choose. It always galls me to hear stylistically 'nineteenth-century' writers like Carver, Ford, Trevor etc. cited as the contemporary masters of the short story form. The sooner Ballard gets the collected stories treatment in three volumes the sooner it will become obvious that his structural and thematic experiments point the way for the form into the twenty-first century. It amazes me that he has written nine books of short stories and that his last is arguably his greatest, the mighty *War Fever*. His use of alphabets, questionnaires etc. showed me that at the end of this century of fragmentation there are sometimes better ways of telling stories than using the old linear model.

**S. R.** What popular cultural influences are there in your fiction?

**M. M.** It is impossible for a writer my age to remain uninfluenced by popular culture. My first idea that movies, TV, comics, rock and roll, etc. were fit material for fiction came about through reading Pynchon, particularly *The Crying of Lot 49*. That small book – another cartoon – is a near seamless weave of jingles, TV shows and rock and roll songs. It is also a lesson on how to create a coherent, heartbreaking narrative out of essentially disposable rubbish. Sam Peckinpah has been an influence of sorts. Because of my love of Westerns I've tried writing 'action sequences' and of course the opening and closing scenes of *The*

*Wild Bunch* have provided me with a kind of stylistic grammar for that kind of thing. The breaking down of continuous movement into its constituent parts is one of my favourite devices. More than that, however, I find Peckinpah's themes of friendship between men who are essentially out of time and step with the world really intriguing.

One of the most worrying influences on my work, and one which my editor claims makes him 'nervous' is heavy metal. Generally speaking a fondness for bands like Black Sabbath, Motorhead, Deep Purple, Maiden, Slayer is something you grow out of in your late teens. I never have and to this day a good part of my listening is taken up with bands working themes of violence, destruction and hard-loving women in the heart of the city. While it is probably the most reviled of all music forms – the excessive machismo, the ludicrous posturing, the bludgeoning sameness of its themes and rhythms – this is not the place to enter a defence. It's too easy to sound ridiculous and is, more to the point, a betrayal of the siege mentality which is so essential to its thriving ghetto existence. A sense of affliction is necessary to any understanding of it. What I will say is that bands like Sabbath, Rainbow and Slayer have contributed as much to my idea of the 'gothic' as have writers such as Poe or scholars like Huizinga or Keith Thomas. It might, in reality, be all bad sword and sorcery but it's a coherent pantheon of wizards, magicians, serial killers and angels of death. As I say, it's probably something I should have grown out of but there you go. To tell the truth I don't care to enquire too deeply into it.

After I left college I shared houses with a succession of visual artists – painters, photographers and sculptors. Their work methods intrigued and fascinated me. Collectors of rubbish and terminally disorganised, they nevertheless took great pains to show me some of the secrets of their work. And the more I learned about their work the more mysterious it all became. What I did learn was how to see colour in all its shadings, gradations and rhythms. Sometimes now when I'm writing descriptive passages I realise that I am imitating some of the techniques they have shown me. A good example of this lies in the opening lines of 'The Angel Of Death'. That brush stroke description of the hero is me fancying myself as a portrait painter.

**S. R.** What projects are you involved in at the moment?

**M. M.** At the moment I'm writing my second novel. So far I'm only about twenty pages into it so I won't say very much about it. I have a policy of never talking about anything I'm writing. I also have this theory that books in progress are like illicit love affairs – the more you talk about them the more likely you are to jeopardise them.

*Duncan McLean*

# Bunker Man
Duncan McLean

*Born in the 1960s, Duncan McLean was brought up in Aberdeenshire.*
*Duncan McLean is author of the novels* Bunker Man *and* Blackden *and*
*the collection of short stories* Bucket of Tongues. *He is a successful*
*playwright and has published a collection of his plays entitled* Plays
One. *He is author of the music and travel writing book* Lone Star Swing
*on Bob Wills and his Texas Playboys.*

   *Duncan McLean won the Somerset Maugham award in 1993 and*
*used the proceeds to travel from Orkney to Texas in 1995 to research*
*'western swing' in the Lone Star State, quickly getting 'On the Trail of*
*Bob Wills and his Texas Playboys' as a fan of the music. McLean –*
*along with his friend and fellow writer James Meek – started* Clocktower
*Press at the beginning of the 1990s and edited an anthology of ten*
*of the* Clocktower *booklets all published between 1990 and 1994 –*
*with additional new writing from Irvine Welsh, Alan Warner, Janice*
*Galloway and James Kelman as well as Duncan McLean himself in*
*a book called, quite correctly,* Ahead Of Its Time. *Duncan gives a*
*succinct potted history of the* Clocktower Press *in the introduction to the*
*anthology entitled* Time Bombs: A Short History of the Clocktower Press.
*He acknowledges that James Meek and himself took 'our inspiration*
*from music and football fanzines' to start* Clocktower Press*: this was a*
*literary 'DIY culture'.*

   *McLean acknowledges satirical comedy as a major influence on his*
*writing. During the mid-1980s he was a member of the very successful*
*satirical comedy group The Merry Macs. He wrote and performed with*
*the fun show. He was also a member of The Comedy Casuals.*

   *Duncan McLean now lives in Orkney, just about as far as it is*
*possible to be in Britain from the southern-based literary establishment.*
*We conversed by e-mail over several weeks.*

**STEVE REDHEAD** Why did you, and how did you, get into writing fiction?

**DUNCAN McLEAN** As a teenager in Aberdeenshire (1980ish) I was heavily into music and wrote songs for the punk band me and my brother and our friend Douglas Rumbles had – The Distorts. We played in a few youth clubs in the area and at the village hall in Torphins. This was country boys' idea of punk based on listening to John Peel and reading the *NME* from a very long distance away. Probably it was pretty funny stuff, highly reminiscent of the rock family tree in Alan Warner's *These Demented Lands*. I've a half-written story about that period called 'Three Chords That Shook The World' which I hope to finish some day. Later on, as a student in Edinburgh (and afterwards on the dole for a year or so) I was still writing songs, and also stand-up comedy and street theatre. I was in a group called the Merry Mac Fun Show which achieved quite a bit of success in the mid-eighties. We were very politically motivated, and very explicit about politics in our material. But despite that we also managed to be funny, and to play just about everywhere from unemployed workers' centres and nightclubs and colleges across the Central Belt, to Highland halls and schools, to radio and television shows including *Wogan*! Surreal. I've another half-written story about all that called 'On The Steps' (title pinched from a Gorky story with the spelling changed).

By spring 1988 the Merry Macs had broken up (as groups tend to do) and I had started four and a half years as a janitor for Edinburgh District Council, first in Princes Street Gardens, and then in South Queensferry. I took this job because it was a good job – small but regular pay, low stress, rent-free flat attached to the hall I looked after – but also because I wanted to try writing fiction seriously. I'd got fed up with the performer's lifestyle, but still wanted to write. And I wanted to write something more like what I was actually reading with great excitement at the time: the fiction of Alasdair Gray, James Kelman and (a bit later) Janice Galloway and Gordon Legge. The janitor's job gave me a lot of free time to read (not to mention watching a lot of daytime TV) and also to write. And that's what I did pretty solidly for the next four years. I made a couple of attempts at a novel, which soon collapsed because I hadn't learned the craft for anything ambitious, then moved on to writing short stories. I'd always liked reading stories, and I found that for a writer trying to find out how prose worked they were ideal: they allowed you to experiment with different tenses, paces, points of view and see the results of the experiments very quickly. I had a Samuel Beckett poster up on the wall with a quotation: 'Try, fail, try again, fail better,' (something like that). Anyway I tried and failed for two years or so, then finally started placing (and even selling – for £20 or so) stories in small magazines in Scotland, England, USA and Canada. I kept on trying and failing better for another couple of years, got a few more magazine publications, did a few readings, finally got a full collection together – *Bucket of Tongues*. By this time I'd got to be friends with quite a few other writers in similar situations to me – James Meek, Robert Alan Jamieson, Gordon Legge – and had even started a small press to publish their work (and my own). I won't go into the history of Clocktower as I've already written about it in more than enough detail in the introduction to *Ahead Of Its Time*, the Clocktower anthology. I will say it was a good time to be starting to write fiction: a lot of great work was going on, and there was a very supportive, encouraging atmosphere amongst the writers I knew. Plus it seemed like every few months another great new voice would emerge in poetry or prose: Jim Ferguson, Alison Kermack, Irvine Welsh. I learned a lot from what the folk I've mentioned were doing, and got a hell of a lot of excitement and stimulation and sustenance out of their work: that's what it's all about.

**S. R.** Who were your other literary influences? What about the Beat Generation for instance, or Charles Bukowski?

**D. M.** I mentioned music and stand-up comedy, and I think it's worthwhile underlining that influences from those areas were as important to me when I started writing as any narrowly defined 'literary' ones. I remember James Meek arguing that contemporary writers were lying if they said their work wasn't influenced by TV and film. I'm sure he's right, but for me it was the DIY ethos of punk that was a real catalyst to getting involved with creative work. And from comedy, the wonderful, scabrous, nihilistic monologues of Jerry Sadowitz influenced me in the late eighties in more specific ways. The way he used words as physical objects, the way he structured his (apparently free-form) rants on multiple levels, the way he used different voices for different effects – all that while still making me sick with laughter – that was an inspiration.

Having said that I've always been a great reader and can certainly point out a few writers or books that have been very important to me over the years. I read *Sunset Song* and most of the rest of Lewis Grassic Gibbon when I was eighteen. That came like a thunderbolt. He was writing about the area I grew up in – right down to individual roads and villages and hills! (*Grey Granite* ends, for instance, on top of the Barmekin Hill about three miles away from where I was sitting reading the book in the summer of 1983.) I've seen Alan Warner say in interviews that, as a teenager, he'd never read any books set in the part of the country he knew. (There's that famous bit in *Lanark* too where it's remarked that no one can imagine living in Glasgow because there's been so little written imaginatively about the place.) Anyone growing up in Aberdeenshire or the Mearns has the fantastic inheritance of the works of Gibbon. His fiction is full of the north-east land and the north-east people and the north-east language. Later on I also came to appreciate some of the ambitious technical innovations that Gibbon was making in his later novels. Because he was Scottish, maybe, or because he died so young, or for a combination of reasons certainly including politics and language, I don't think Gibbon's ever got the recognition he deserves as a very daring 'Modernist'. His work was being published at the same time as Joyce, Kafka, Eliot and Woolf, and he should certainly be considered in that company, rather than relegated to a Scotch peasant backwater.

About six months later, maybe January 1984, I got hit by another thunderbolt: James Kelman's *The Busconductor Hines*. I'd read some of *Not Not While The Giro* but it was really *Hines* that took me into Kelman's work in a big way. In fact I'd already read and enjoyed *Lanark* by this time too but it was *Hines* that really excited me, and alerted me to the the fact that there were folk writing now about the place I lived in right now. In the same way that Gibbon was writing about a place

I knew, Kelman was writing about a time I knew: I recognised the people, the language, the predicaments, the politics, the culture, the world. Of course Kelman's a great writer in all sorts of ways. But for me, and no doubt a lot of other writers who have been published in the last ten years or so, he was more than that. Kelman was the first contemporary I was aware of who made fiction seem like a necessary thing, like a vital thing, like something I should get involved with. I won't talk about other influences at nearly so much length. Simply because, without denying the significance to me of many other writers, I believe it is Gibbon and Kelman who were by far the most important literary influences on everything I've done and am likely to do.

Amongst the others I must mention though are: James Hogg (above all *Justified Sinner* but many of the realistic short stories of country life are real gems. *Bunker Man* is essentially a 1990s reworking of *Justified Sinner* by the way, though nobody seems to have noticed except for me!); Turgenev's novels, especially *Fathers and Sons*; Chekhov's stories but not his plays; Tolstoy for his clarity of vision and voice; Guy de Maupassant, who did just about everything that can be done with the short story form – his *Bel Ami* is a great novel too; and Bohumil Hrabal, Knut Hamsun, Flaubert, Gholam Hussein Sai 'di, Lu Xun, Dickens.

You mention the Beat Generation in your question, and there's been some daft stuff written about the 'Scottish Beats' etc., so I think I should take this opportunity to say that – with the sole exception of *Howl* which is a good rant in the Jerry Sadowitz mould – none of the Beat Generation writing does anything for me at all. In fact I've read very little of it. I much prefer the American writers of a generation earlier like Damon Runyon, Ring Lardner, Katherine Anne Porter and even Hemingway. It's Hemingway's stories I like, by the way. I think you can see the influence of *Big Two-Hearted River* on my own *Hours Of Darkness* (though the title for that came from the Gram Parsons country song *In My Hour Of Darkness*). By the way I think you can see the influence of *Hours Of Darkness* on the first section of Alan Warner's *These Demented Lands*! Speaking of Alan Warner, that reminds me that I should mention the fact that a lot of my contemporaries – especially, perhaps, James Meek, Robert Alan Jamieson, Alison Kermack, Janice

Galloway – have influenced me a lot by things they've said. I mean I've talked for hours about books and writing and politics and life with all of them for hours and hours and often found what they've said has been inspiring or educational or provocative. The funny thing is, although I admire their work enormously, I think it's their conversation that has actually influenced me. The only influence I'm aware of from one of my contemporaries when I sit down to write is Alan Warner. I'm not sure why. Maybe because he shares a similar rural background. I don't know.

You mention Charles Bukowski. I first read him in about 1990, on holiday in Torremolinos. I found *The Most Beautiful Woman in the World* in a secondhand shop. I enjoyed it a hell of a lot and tracked down as much as I could by him as soon as I got back home. I think he wrote a lot of good stories, and a few good novels – *Factotum* is my favourite – but in the end I think he's pretty limited. I mean he goes over the same territory again and again and again. That gets boring after a while. I prefer writers who are continually stretching themselves – and their readers. My eye was caught by the Bukowski book in Spain because I'd seen his name in a poem by Raymond Carver, and that reminds me that in Carver's essay about his influences – I think it's called 'Fires' – he cites his children! They influenced him more than any other writer because they just made it so hard for him to write for years! Of course he's right: no one's a writer 100% of the time, they're a human being a hundred per cent of the time and a writer whenever they sit down to read or think or write – maybe twenty per cent of their time? So the real influences on Duncan McLean are not Bukowski and Warner, or even Gibbon and Kelman – they're only influences on McLean the Writer – no, the real influences are the weather in Orkney, the road system in the northern Highlands, Mad Cow disease, the Single European Currency and the price of cheese in Sanday. But that's another story.

**S. R.** What popular cultural influences (music, films) are there on your writing style or content?

**D. M.** Your question's difficult, or maybe troubling. I'm not confident it's possible to define 'popular' culture, as opposed to any other sort of culture. Putting that objection to one side: I've already mentioned

Jerry Sadowitz, the comedian. There were probably other stand-ups and street performers who impressed me a lot too – The Redheads from Glasgow, The Vulcans from London. As you know I've written a book *Lone Star Swing* about Texas music – in particular western swing. I love the stuff, but don't think you could reasonably say it has much 'influence' on my fiction. The same goes for film, TV etc. I watch as much as anyone, but very little of it really grabs me. About the only stuff I feel I could specifically mention is the work of Alan Clarke e.g. *Scum, The Firm, Elephant* – and some of Ken Loach e.g. *Kes, My Name Is Joe* and a few in between. And Laurel and Hardy.

**S. R.** How far have fanzines and other independent publishing been influential on you? Do you think that literary fanzines have taken over from football- and music-based ones which have perhaps now lost their force?

**D. M.** The fanzine scene – whether in literature, football or music (where I first encountered the notion) – goes right back to the punk aesthetic of my youth. What I take from punk and fanzines is: who cares about big production values, glossy covers, technical flashiness, million dollar deals? What art is really about is finding an outlet for your voice, for your culture. It could be in a sonnet cycle or a sonata, if that's the culture you're coming from, but it could just as well be a two-minute two-chord song, or a one-paragraph story. I'll tell you about the 'zines that were important to me, and really got me thinking about starting *Clocktower*. Probably nobody knows this. (Let's face it, probably nobody cares about this! And why should they? But I might as well set it down while I have the chance, ha ha.) They were American and Canadian, mostly, and I found out about them through a catalogue-type publication called *Factsheet Five* published in the States – full of hundreds and hundreds of two-sentence reviews/descriptions of 'zines on different topics, from music to sex to fiction to food to neglected body parts. I scraped together some dollar bills (they usually only cost a dollar or two) and bought quite a few. They had titles like *Hippo*, *Onionhead* and *Lost*. On the whole they were very badly produced – poor photocopies, carelessly stapled, of badly typed fiction and badly drawn cartoons. But that didn't matter. What mattered is that they sparked with wild ideas and raw emotion. The fiction was often crude, but always exciting. Like a Patrick Fitzgerald record. Or like the early *Clocktower* booklets, which were really just Scottish versions of the American 'zines. Having said all that, I don't see any point in glorifying the publications at the expense of the writing. *Clocktower* itself is nothing, it's the writing it helped encourage and promote – by Alison Kermack, Irvine Welsh, Alan Warner, James Meek – that's the important thing. Or at least it's the interesting thing. Likewise I'm very glad that *Rebel Inc* existed, but not because of the magazine itself, just because it was a vehicle which brought me great writing by Laura Hird, John King and other folk I'd never heard of. If you want me to really answer your question, I should at least mention the last part of it, where you imply that literary 'zines have 'taken over' some of the 'lost force' of football and music ones. Well, I haven't seen a new *Rebel Inc* for a long time and *Clocktower*'s only put out one booklet in the last two years (though that was an exceptionally good one – Simon Crump's 'My Elvis Blackout'). The particular bunch of writers who first came to wider attention through those fugitive publications have, on the whole, either graduated to other, paying, forms of print, or else have come to their senses and got proper jobs. So I don't think the literary 'zines have taken over anything at all. But as I said above, who cares? Most periodicals should be put out of their misery after three or four years anyway. It's extremely depressing to see certain literary magazines struggling on year after year, their main claim to fame being, not that they're publishing anything interesting since 1983, but that they're *still surviving* despite cuts in grants, falling subscriptions etc. etc., like some old codger waving his stick and mumbling 'I'm ninety-two you know!'

**S. R.** What do you think of today's political culture? Does your writing and other 'new fiction' have any connection to it?

**D. M.** The eighties was a very interesting decade, politically – full of unrest, turmoil and confrontation. I think it'll be looked back on as a period of extraordinary conflict in the history of the UK state. To name the most obvious examples of this, there was the Falklands War, the anti poll-tax movement, many race-related riots across the country and (this being one that galvanised me more than anything) the Miners' Strike.

And always underneath all that there was the constant gloating greed of the upper middle classes and their government, and the relentless impoverishing of whole swathes of society – mostly the most vulnerable parts of it. And if you were living in Scotland there was another constant undercurrent: unhappiness and frustration at the collusion of Labour and the Tories to deny the population here their democratically-expressed will – i.e. political self-determination. I was born towards the end of 1964 and so by the time I was becoming aware of politics Thatcher was in power and the kind of conflict I outline above was starting to surface more and more. Living through that for most of my adult life has influenced me profoundly – of course. Having said that all about the eighties, I think it's worth underlining that there's political conflict in every era, everywhere, including here and now. For the past few years the conflict has maybe subsided a bit, or maybe it's just been pushed under the carpet. But it's there all the same, in the depths of the whole UK set up, in the depths of the whole misogynistic, racist, imperialist, misanthropic capitalist set up. In my opinion, anyone who denies that is kidding themselves. I can understand why some folk want to kid themselves: it probably makes life a lot easier and more comfortable to pretend everything out there's jim dandy. (Of course you have to have a certain amount of security, a certain amount of callousness and a certain amount of *cash* to be able to pull off this self-deception convincingly.) But any writer who tries to kid himself or herself that the world they live in and write about isn't riven with conflict is doomed to creating second-rate work. It might be an interesting technical exercise, but it's as limited as writing a novel that pretends there's only day and no night. Happily, most of the authors of what you call the 'new fiction' of recent times keep their eyes open to the realities. One of the reasons there's been so much good stuff coming out of Scotland over the past ten or fifteen years is because writers have been telling stories about the world as it is, not as they'd like it to be. There's a huge variety of styles and angles and approaches evident in the work of contemporary Scottish writers but just about all of it is underpinned by that philosophy. It's the same philosophy that underpins Tolstoy, Chaucer, Lu Xun, Chekhov – everybody who's any good. You can't write with your eyes closed.

*Jeff Noon*

# **Dub Fiction**
Jeff Noon

Jeff Noon was born in the 1960s and has lived most of his life in Manchester. He is author of the novels Vurt, Pollen, Automated Alice, Nymphomation *and an original collection of fifty of his short stories,* Pixel Juice.

Noon contributed 'DJNA' to Disco Biscuits *and 'Latitude 52' to* Intoxication. *A 'new wave' musician, painter and Writer-in-Residence at the Royal Exchange Theatre in Manchester in the 1980s, in the 1990s he has pushed 'cyberfiction' to new limits. The eventually closed for good (maybe, definitely) Hacienda nightclub hosted Jeff Noon first nights for his novels, and a local publisher, Ringpull, published* Vurt *and* Pollen *before going bust. The* New Statesman *called* Vurt *'too beautiful for bikers, too harsh for hippies'. Certainly Jeff Noon takes 'cyberpunk' from William Gibson et al and whacks into another plane altogether.*

By mid-1999 he was no longer resident in the 'rainy city' and has long bemoaned the fact that for all its pop culture production and cultural regeneration projects, café bars and clubs, Manchester has failed to energise all that much new writing. He's possibly right, though listings magazine City Life *has published two supplements of Manchester writers' short stories and also put out a bumper* Book of Manchester Short Stories *in association with Penguin. So things are certainly changing in the streets of Anthony Burgess and* A Clockwork Orange.

Jeff Noon now lives in Brighton but to date Manchester is the backbone of his cyberscience fiction stories even if it is a futuristic cityscape we're talking here. His final 'Manchester' novel, Needle In The Groove, *is based on the post-war music history of the city. Of his 'dub fiction' the best example is* Cobralingus.

I talked with Jeff Noon at one of Manchester's new café bars before he gave a reading from Pixel Juice.

**STEVE REDHEAD** What were your influences? Were there science fiction writers in this area before?

**JEFF NOON** The thing is, they did exist before, just that nobody noticed them. I'm specifically referring to Philip K. Dick. I came of age in the 1970s, when there was seemingly nothing to read except for McEwan, Amis, Angela Carter – that crowd. I certainly wasn't reading Philip K. Dick. I'd heard of him, but just thought he was a hippie writer i.e. a sixties writer, and therefore nothing to do with me. But if you actually look at his career, he was writing books right through the seventies, into the early eighties, when he died (in 1982). Okay, he wrote *Do Androids Dream* in 1964, but he wrote *Flow My Tears, the Policeman Said* in 1974. And *A Scanner Darkly* in 1977, which makes it a punk novel! Both of these are prime drug/youth culture texts. I never read this stuff at the time, and more importantly, it wasn't being reviewed, not even by papers like the *New Musical Express*. And there were no other ways of finding out about such things at the time, no *Face*, *Arena*, *GQ* etc. So how were we supposed to know this work was interesting? Maybe there are other sixties writers who got ignored in the same way, once the seventies started.

**S. R.** Although you have written about club and pop culture the actual techniques – dub, mixing, etc. – are being transformed into writing techniques in some of your fiction aren't they?

**J. N.** In *Pixel Juice* I went for lots of different voices and effects and lots of different language along with some extremely real stories which is something I haven't really presented to people before, you know. It was a real way of stretching out, really good to write. Most of them are written especially for it so I'm hoping it's not your usual short story collection and that I've got a real feel to the whole thing. It's fragmented by its very nature but I've kind of weaved in lots of different weird connections between the stories and I hope that works. Also I have broken it down it four sections. In my mind at least there's a kind of hidden narrative behind the stories. Some of the stories deal with drugs or the club culture thing which is not the only thing I do. 'Orgmentations' from *Pixel Juice* is a short story which leads into 'Hands of the DJ' which is a long story. What I've done is I've mixed two, I've segued the stories. You'll see that this is the most advanced bit of that I've done in the book. It's early days yet I must admit for this sort of stuff. 'Homo Karaoke' is set in the club world and is a kind of weird DJ story but what I've done here is I've done a dub. You'll get this quite a few times in the book. This is 'Dub Karaoke (Electric Haiku Remix)'. Basically I go through the story and I take out images that hit me and then I get them on the screen and then I jumble them all up and then I start to look at them. Now there's something really interesting happened here because I was just messing about with the images and I got these two and it took me a while before it hit me what I'd done, I'd quite subconsciously set them out as 'haikus' – perfect 'haikus' in the sense that it's five, seven and five syllables. I thought, bloody hell that's pretty good. Whenever I'm doing something like that you're trying to find a form out of the experimentation and that takes a while. They're very sparse on the page. You've got to get it just right. When you chisel it down like that. In stories you're more going for the burn.

Another story in *Pixel Juice* is called 'Metaphorazine' which I hope is going to be one of my 'greatest hits'! This is based on a couple of government reports that you've been reading about, one of which is saying that young people are taking more and more drugs and the other is that young people don't read as much and they're not learning the finer points of English grammar etc. at school – which is very worrying for me especially as I'm very concerned about words and that. So I thought why not combine the two problems so this is a kind of fun piece – it's a kind of 'chemical generation' guide to the English language. It goes down great in performances.

**S. R.** How is music itself connected to what you're writing about?

**J. N.** Science fiction is the most obvious genre to portray this dance generation thing in the sense that I think, say, a Goldie record for instance, I actually consider that to be science fiction not about science fiction – although very often it is about science fiction, specifically comic book heroes, but it actually *is* science fiction. And what I noticed is that there are certain correlations between what say the cyberpunk of William Gibson introduced into science fiction with what the record producers and the DJs were doing with the equipment. Specifically – I mean I don't want to go too far into it this – but the cyberpunk literary movement introduced the idea that science would be inside us, that there would be an invasion, an infection, of science and I use that over and over again. What I thought was happening with music, with the sampling for instance, is that one music is infecting another music, is stealing things off it like a virus. And I thought well this is quite interesting and 'hasn't anybody out there kind of noticed this?' and I thought I can use this. So one of the images I use again and again and again is the idea that music is a kind of parasite, it takes people over, specifically it's a drug, you can inject it say, so instead of listening to a record, you become records. In *Pixel Juice* there's tons of things like that, about that, the infection by the music. So I'm thinking of things like dub, if you break down the actual techniques that are being used in music and let's just say at the beginning most of them weren't invented by or for dance music. They've been around since like 1910, and classical music. My actual physical interest in dance music is tiny. I have lots of different interests in music and I love music but I love classical music as well. The techniques have been used, what dance music has done is given them names: sampling, scratching, mixing, remixing, dub etc. etc. It isn't something I've sat down and said I'm gonna do this, it's kind of infected me in a way. I'm very interested in language in a way that I hope that I get across in the actual form itself, this kind of infection that's going on.

**S. R.** Is your fiction about youth culture, about 'rites of passage' in any way?

**J. N.** I went through the usual puberty thing with science fiction and I don't really think that anybody's looked at science fiction and puberty yet and they should do because there's obviously a big connection there and I also see it as being connected with surrealism, you know. As an adolescent lad I was tremendously excited by these burning giraffes and things like that and there's obviously something sexual going on there that you can't really work out. I think it's the same with science fiction, there's a sexual element there. I kind of put science fiction aside and then came back with William Gibson and read *Neuromancer* and that was the spark for me. The first page of *Neuromancer* was just such a rush and a charge. You couldn't help but be excited by it and obviously the cog had turned here, the ratchet had gone round, 'yeah wow something's happening'. The other person very, very powerfully important to me is JG Ballard, so in between discovering Gibson I did JG Ballard and I've read everything by Ballard, I absolutely adore Ballard.

**S. R.** What other influences did you have apart from music and writers?

**J. N.** Painting. That's what I could do as a kid and I always have studied that and I always did that and I did that at college. I went to Thameside College of Technology to do my A levels in painting and sculpture. There I met this guy, a teacher Bill Clark, who completely turned everything I thought I knew about art around. Specifically, what he would say to us was 'that's great, that painting's fine, but now I want you to destroy it. I want you to cut that painting up and re-use it in other ways'. So we were getting the scissors out and cutting things up and sticking them down and starting again. And you would introduce a lot of techniques like that. This had nothing to do with music as far as he was concerned. To him it was just a way of releasing the creativity. To a sixteen or seventeen year-old at first it's a shock. But then for a few of us it was a tremendous liberation.

What happened at the same time, 1976, 1977, was that punk came out. Now I was, I got heavily involved in the whole punk thing. Looking back punk destroyed more than it did good. But one very special thing happened, which is that white kids were introduced to dub reggae. Now to me, that's it. If you can take the idea of dub reggae and merge it with the things I was learning about painting at college I think you'll find that I am still using those techniques in my writing. I mean the first dub reggae I heard wasn't even dub reggae, it was The Clash's 'Police and Thieves'. But I was amazed by the space, the emptiness that was being left there. If you're doing a dub of a story, this is the real story – I mean even just physically to look at it – that's the song, this is the dub. There's only a few words there, because they're the best bits.

**S. R.** What about musical involvement. You played in bands didn't you?

**J. N.**  Yeah, I played in bands. New wave rather than punk. To me new wave is punk plus dub reggae. We were using space and it was all very brittle and fragmented like it was at the time. I suppose XTC was the classic band that were doing that sort of stuff, cos they were doing dub experiments, they did some really good ones actually. I was doing lots of different things. I kind of moved around a lot and had lots of different jobs. I went to do my BA actually quite late in life. And I decided to do combined arts, painting and drama. What happened before that was out of Thameside College of Technology we started this group called Stand and Deliver. Started by Mike Rook at the college. He used to do something called liberal arts. Now I don't know whether they do liberal arts anymore. But what it was, it was a College of Technology so it was filled with artists but it was also filled with domestic science, engineering, hairdressing students but by some perverse kind of logic everybody in the college had to do one hour of liberal arts with Mike Rook. That introduced me to a whole load of other things because I'd gone there to paint, I was a serious painter in those days, I was oil on the canvas. What he did was introduce us to writing and playing and making up things and having games and improvising. I started to write poetry and I started to perform it live with Stand and Deliver. And slowly the poems became more and more dramatic so they became like little mini plays where I was thinking of lots of characters.

So when I did go to college I studied painting and drama, hoping to combine the two – it didn't in fact happen and at the end of that I decided that it was time to concentrate and I was going to just choose one thing so I threw the music away. I actually threw the painting away too. I haven't painted since 1984. I decided to write plays. Just before I left college I'd come up with this cracker of an idea for a play called *Woundings* which went on to win a prize – that's just been filmed actually. Then I was at the Royal Exchange. I thought I was a playwright. It turned out in fact I wasn't. I had go through some kind of soul searching before I came to the conclusion that I wasn't a playwright. I was desperately trying to get a second play on. I'd been involved in the whole fringe scene. I didn't want to go back to that. Nobody was interested in a second play of mine. About ten years

I was writing plays. I started to work at Waterstone's on Deansgate to support myself. *Vurt* took about a year to write. Steve Powell, who worked at Waterstone's and started Ringpull Press, started me writing *Vurt*. He asked me to write a book because he liked my plays. And that's how it came about.

**S. R.** How did it help you working with a small, independent local publisher like Ringpull?

**J. N.** The first two books were tremendously well edited. They were written very intimately. Steve Powell and I worked on them very intimately together. It was a very rigorous process that we went through. But I don't know. It's a kind of a personal thing that hit me because when it went bankrupt I did lose a lot of money. It's a double-edged sword that whole independent thing. I know it's happened to other people and I've talked to other writers and it happens. Then I went to Transworld Publishers with the finished draft of *Automated Alice* and the idea for *Nymphomation*.

**S. R.** This was 1994, the year of the Criminal Justice and Public Order Act. Were you aware of legal and social regulation of the culture that you had started to write fiction about?

**J. N.** Certainly when I was writing *Vurt* none of that 'Repetitive Beat' law had come in. If you look at *Vurt* the actual dance culture thing in it is minute. There's one scene set in a disco. But I know when people read that book I had a lot of people coming up to me saying 'Jeff I love that scene. Nobody's done that before'. I wasn't really that conscious of it. I was looking round Manchester and thinking what have we got here, we've got these young people on the streets, we've got the drugs, we've got the music, we've got the guns. At the time there was all that killing going on, on the streets. I was writing a book about Manchester and it had to have that in it. From then I've kind of extended it a little bit. Just like Irvine Welsh claims *Trainspotting* is set in the 1980s – I mean friends of mine who have read *Vurt* and have known me for a number of years have said 'Jeff you set it in 1977'. Some people think it's set in 1977 with the whole punk thing. Other people think it's about contemporary nineties Manchester. But in fact it's set in the future. So I'm kind of playing these games with where exactly is this book set. It's like present day Manchester but it's been infected by these certain elements of the future. I am, with the *Vurt* books, trying to create an overall feel but they're not in any sense sequels. It's not that rigorous with my work. I like to talk about a web of connections between my work. There's little images and mirror images which will maybe resonate in people's minds – in individual books but also across the books.

**S. R.** In this period Manchester has claimed to be a 'world city' regenerating itself through 'European' culture and café bars whilst you've been writing its possible future in fiction. What do you actually think of it?

**J. N.** I was talking to Nick Blincoe the other night. And he was saying that his book is about Manchester [*Manchester Slingback*] and how much it has changed and that he kept coming back and it improved. Now, whether Manchester has actually improved is a moot point as far as I'm concerned. Putting up some café bars and some warmed up ciabatta bread does not make a European city. Sorry, it doesn't. There's still a tremendous number of problems here. To me the most shameful problem is the suicide rate of young men. I mean it's the highest in the country and all the café bars in the world mean nothing against that.

I like to twist the question around and I like to say what is it about Manchester that is making its young men kill themselves? And that's a question that's not being asked. Michael Bracewell writes about this in his book *Pop Life in Albion* in the chapter 'Lucifer over Lancashire'. I mean, he's one of the only people who has gone into that. And if you go back into Manchester music, obviously in the early days you had a tremendous darkness in the music. With all this thing that's going on in Manchester, with all this change and the European thing coming in, that darkness is still there but it's not being used. We've got Oasis, a band without an ounce of darkness unless you consider a v-sign to be darkness! Where's that darkness going? So I suppose in *Nymphomation* Manchester is a lot different from the other books. It is a more conglomerate thing. There are more little mini conspiracies going on.

*Elaine Palmer*

# Pulp Faction
Elaine Palmer

*Elaine Palmer was born in the 1960s in London and grew up in Dublin.*

*She and others started* Pulp Faction *collections of short contemporary fiction in 1994. The likes of* Skin, Techno Pagan, The Living Room, Allnighter, 5 Uneasy Pieces, Fission *and* Random Factor *in the intervening years have all contained sharp, challenging fiction and showcased writers like Joe Ambrose, Nicholas Blincoe, Jeff Noon, Duncan Mclean, Steve Aylett, P-P Hartnett, Alistair Gentry and many more. The logical related venture – novels from Pulp Books – followed several years later.*

*Jeff Noon has described* Pulp Faction *as the 'publishing equivalent of an independent record label' and the same could be said of Pulp Books. Select magazine saw the whole enterprise as proving that 'literary life on these shores does extend beyond Irvine Welsh'. As editor Elaine Palmer argues '* Pulp Faction *has always been very practice rather than theory based'.*

*The graphic style of* Pulp Faction *editions is deliberately derived from fanzines and the covers and layout of* Pulp Books *are all strikingly original and evocative of their contemporary 90s subject matter, mood and writing style. Collections of black fiction – in* Afrobeat *– and fiction on blurred gender – in* Girlboy *– as well as several single authored new novels have been published by Pulp Books. Acclaimed performance artist Tim Etchells, of Sheffield's Forced Entertainment, has recently had his 'state of the end of the millennium nation' book published by Pulp Books. Another Pulp Book, Jon Buscall's* College.com *was submitted, accepted and edited via e-mail.*

*Elaine Palmer lives in London. We conversed by e-mail over several weeks.*

**STEVE REDHEAD** How did you start *Pulp Faction* and Pulp Books?

**ELAINE PALMER** *Pulp Faction*'s first publication *Skin* was put together in 1994 and published in early 1995. Its main motivation was to shove two fingers at the publishing establishment which had rejected pretty much everything in it and to do something with the attitude of a fanzine but that wouldn't get thrown out as quickly. *Time Out* (about the only place to review it) called *Skin* 'essential toilet reading'. I think we kept going after that more because we'd had a good launch party than because it was an instant bestseller. We blagged donations including free beer and and a free venue and people mysteriously arrived at this deserted basement gallery near Old Street. We even got the ultimate accolade – groupies! Pulp Books started closer to 1997, as a kind of logical step forward after a few collections of short fiction. If anyone on the team had rich parents it might have started with more of a splash but in fact it started with just one book *Call Me* by P-P Hartnett. This book has now sold out several printings in Britain and been published in the USA and Germany. We've also published P-P Hartnett's second novel *I Want To Fuck You* – in 1998 – which five printers both from within and outside the UK refused to work on because of its title. It was a great one to have to say to journalists on the phone, but it frightened most of them off as well though it did get a mention from Will Self in the *Times*.

**S. R.** How and why did you get into fiction?

**E. P.** I had a varied writing, editing and production background mainly acquired as a freelance in cheesy magazines, but my only fiction editing before *Pulp Faction* was a fanzine called *Nightboat*, produced from a squat some years earlier. Luckily I don't have any copies of this left because I have an idea there was some seriously *bad* poetry in there by a very pretty blond boy from the squat next to mine. Knowing how to do stuff from cheesy magazines was useful, but the fanzine experience was a big part of it. I am not lying when I say I don't have a copy of *Nightboat*. The fanzine ethic comes over pretty clearly in the *Pulp Faction* collections – at a visual level, lots of images and very chaotic typesetting style for a book. But to come back to what it is about fanzines that's useful: two main things I think. One is that your friends are going to be your worst critics because you care what they think so if you can recover from a slagging off by them (and believe me Dubliners treat slagging as an art form – a huge cultural difference from Southern England where the worst insult is silence or politeness) then you have nothing left to fear. And the other is the joy of finishing something, getting it out and not caring if it sells. Like bands paying to press their first single (I think Nirvana actually paid for their first album) it's just a way of proving that you believe in what you're doing even if no one else does.

**S. R.** What literary influences did you have? What about the beat generation for instance? Or Charles Bukowski?

**E. P.** I was born in London but spent my teenage years in Dublin, so James Joyce was a big influence. (Finally gave up reading *Ulysses* at my sixth attempt when I realised he was the one who'd lost the plot. But the style was bloody good.) I remember meeting Seamus Heaney who visited our school when I was in fifth form and Brendan Kennelly who I used to bump into in a pub somewhere just after I'd left school. The thing I liked about meeting writers was getting drunk at their events, which beat art receptions for laughs because the writers were into meeting people and telling stories. But what I really wanted to do back then was movies and I went off and starred in an obscure road movie or two of my own round Europe before coming back to London and starting over. But the beats? No, please. I remember one or two people whose musical taste I went along with telling me how great Kerouac/Bukowski and co were. So then they'd lend me the books and I'd give them back and say, this is crap. I mean the 'women' stuff in those books is *so-o* bad it's embarrassing: 'then I fucked another one and she somehow failed to notice that I was just some boring up-his-own-arse waster'. I've worked with one or two writers who name the beats, or at least Burroughs, as an influence. Joe Ambrose (*Serious Time* and *Too Much Too Soon*) – actually not sure who else. Maybe Tim Etchells (*Endland Stories*). With Burroughs, he sort of preceded the technology because lots of culture is cut-up now. I'm thinking of movies, TV programmes, trailers, retrospectives, channel-hopping etc. so you can appreciate that kind of thing without ever having read or been directly influenced by his take on cut-up. Visual pop culture like film, TV and music videos have really cross-fertilised modern writing, undermining the whole necessity for givens like three-act structure, conventional resolution etc. But as always the places where writing is taught and the places where it's bought have tended to lag behind.

Other literary influences: James Baldwin, Douglas Coupland, Colin Wilson (the early fiction), Jean Luc Godard. Films generally have been a huge influence on the writing I like. Stuff like *Frisk* by Dennis Cooper works because we're so familiar with movies. With *Trainspotting* I couldn't read the book until after I'd seen the film, because my Scottish isn't good enough. But that's a different thing. Other influences? Laurie Anderson, KLF (the music not the book), Klaus Nomi for mucking with genres – the first to mix opera and punk – the Stone Roses, music that combines optimism and negativity, Nirvana, Stereolab, Asian Dub Foundation. I had an e-chat with Alistair Gentry who I've been working with off and on for a few years now. I've published his short stories and novel *Their Heads Are Anonymous* – his second novel called *Monkey Boys* is on our current catalogue. I mentioned to Alistair in an e-mail about something else about the 'chemical generation' thing and I said I was worried I'd been slagging off Bukowski when he might not be considered a 'True Beat' by the diehards. Anyway some of Alistair's comments were quite interesting especially this which probably applies to other writers I'm working with: 'the influence of everything, of constant input, of our culture is very evident in my writing. I'm just as influenced (or not) by adverts, lazy style mag journalism, the nonsense you find on the Net, Jacobean drama, junk mail, pub geniuses, observation, whatever, everything'. Alistair Gentry's *Their Heads Are Anonymous* in particular I feel fits the cultural resistance theory well.

**S. R.** Is some fiction in the 90s part of a resistance to mainstream culture – as perhaps music or other art forms have sometimes been in the last twenty or thirty years?

**E. P.** I tried something like this out on a music journalist who was interested in *Pulp Faction* (he said he didn't otherwise read fiction, but liked our stuff). My theory was that with the most inventive kind of music at present (dance) being essentially without lyrics (or with fragmented, sampled vocals), that break up of narrative in music makes fiction a relatively more interesting area to work. Actually where I work is mostly a music studio (there's someone drumming in the studio underneath right now!) and compared to us the musicians who pass through (most of whom have deals with major labels) are really part of the corporate structure. Anyway this music journo e-mailed his mates in a mini-survey of about ten people and a few people thought 'yeah' but others not. Even strongly disagreeing. Several of the authors I've been working with have some kind of music background and/or arts background. I generally try to avoid working with people who've studied English. When we set up *Pulp Faction* I got really annoyed at people who wrote and said they were at or had just been to Oxford and expected me to jump at the chance of working with them – I mean they could spell and even write incredibly complex, grammatically correct sentences, but didn't necessarily have anything interesting to write about. I remember rejecting a book by a guy like this because it was so much like what was already in the shops. So the next year it came out with Faber and Faber and got great reviews. Wonder how it would have fared with Pulp Books? Oh well, life goes on, and things change very slowly.

*Alan Warner*

# Celtic Trails
Alan Warner

*Alan Warner was born in the mid-1960s and grew up in rural west of Scotland near Oban. He is the author of three highly acclaimed novels:* Morvern Callar, These Demented Lands *and* The Sopranos. *He contributed to the anthology* Disco Biscuits *and has stories in the anthologies* Children of Albion Rovers *and* Ahead Of Its Time.

*Warner has been elevated by a number of critics alongside Irvine Welsh as an outstanding new fiction writer, quite rightly as far as readers are concerned on the evidence of his first three novels. The listings magazine* Time Out *thought that 'he defines the 90s as clearly as Jay McInerney defined the 80s'. His first novel* Morvern Callar *won a Somerset Maugham Award and is soon to be filmed by the young Scottish director Lynn Ramsay. His second novel* These Demented Lands *won an Encore award and his third novel* The Sopranos *the Saltire prize. The film rights for* The Sopranos *have been sold in Hollywood to the Scottish director Michael Caton-Jones (director of* Scandal, This Boy's Life *and* Rob Roy*). Alan Warner has made a CD,* Soundclash, *with the Scottish band Superstar and is a supporter of the German saxophonist Peter Brotzmann for whom he writes sleevenotes.*

*Despite his initial hesitation to be interviewed for this book (feeling that he had little in common with many of the other writers) Alan Warner reveals many of the crucial traits and influences which make up the 'repetitive beat generation' writers' culture. He was an outsider working on the railways and, until he became involved with the underground literary press in the early 1990s, had no outlet for what Duncan McLean has called his 'completely original talent'.*

*Alan Warner now lives in Dublin. We e-mailed each other over several weeks.*

**STEVE REDHEAD** How did you get into fiction? Was it a way of telling contemporary history better?

**ALAN WARNER** Politically this is what happens to me. You do an interview with the *Independent* or something, you talk about Malcolm Lowry, have a few pints, talk about Scottish poetry for one hour. You say 'Hey, I'll get another round in, I've just got a cheque for ten grand' and when the article comes out, there isn't a mention of *one* thing you said about art, or poetry, or writing: just 'Warner slumps in the corner of the bar talking eloquently – Drinks for everyone I've just got a cheque for a hundred thousand grand – he roars'. It's interesting what you say about this currently fashionable view of history, probably 'best' represented in that terrible *Altered State* book. You see I'm amazed how the Criminal Justice and Public Order Act suddenly rates up there with the many forms of oppression and foreign policy crimes the British establishment are carrying out (check out current night curfews on kids in certain Glasgow estates). I think there is a real reactionary danger that contemporary social historians, who pride themselves on being in touch with the street culture and oral history, are producing an inauthentic historical picture that is becoming as inward looking and self-referential as the worst bourgeois history of Great Men. Once we had the history of Napoleon and Gladstone instead of the details of working-class nineteenth-century struggle and affiliation. Now we're getting the history of fashionable 12″ singles, instead of Great Men, which is claiming to be the history of the people. I fear this is in fact the history of a few, privileged media figures/liggers and whatever you say, only a small proportion of the British population. Where is the social history of Handbag House or just the normal drink-laden Saturday night discos that have gone on, unchanged throughout the entire musical changes of the late 1980s and 1990s? There is a snob status going on, that somehow the (politically reactionary or at best indifferent) clubculture shown in *Altered State* is *valid* history but everything else is not. That *Altered State* book soon reached the inevitable *reductio ad absurdem* of trying to say Britain changed when a certain 12″ single came out.

We are dealing here with subjective history of such a level, all our Marx and Engels paperbacks from the 1980s are curling up at the corners in horror! It is history sanctioned and authorised by *The Face* magazine. I think the emphasis on popular music has become a red herring anyway. Popular music has become such a tool in 1990s monopoly capitalism while an entire underground, experimental musical movement in orchestral and free jazz is denied coverage. People like to pretend an avant-garde doesn't exist anymore in so called post-modern culture, so they can be lazy and walk to Virgin and buy tame old shit, but an underground avant-garde really does exist and, as always, mainstream culture draws on it quickly. Aesthetically you have to keep moving faster to avoid being drawn into mannerisms. I think it's this formal/linguistic area of interaction that needs to be studied and talked about in contemporary writing rather than endlessly name-dropping and harping on about that Bukowski guy that everyone reads, or William bloody Burroughs and all Bono's other favourite writers. In other words it *is* the *words* on the page, what they are saying and how they are saying it that we need to look at, rather than subject matter, pop culture references etc. We should talk in *formal* terms of our writing and how we arrived at our styles, because if we don't have style all we have is content and cardboard cut-out of characterisation. I don't think you can get *into* writing; you have to get into reading first. The two have to be inseparable, though my friend Albert French claims not to read at all and has written some fine novels like *I Can't Wait On God* and *Holly*.

I got into reading when I was fifteen. I grew up (1964–1984) in the countryside around Oban, a small highland town on the west coast; very beautiful place, rained a lot, some fishing and tourism, lots of seasonal unemployment. I had a smart mate in fifth year at the High School who was steadily stealing the library, Adidas bag by Adidas bag from the storerooms. Somehow he managed to persuade me to swap some good albums for a bunch of fusty smelling books with the library stamp on them. I found myself with less albums to listen to, a bunch of books and a vague sense of moral improvement. With more time on my hands ('cos I'd less bloody albums), I forced myself through biographies of Scott and Wordsworth but then *Doctor Faustus* by Thomas Mann, Herman Hesse's *Glass Bead Game*, *The Dalkey Archive* by Flann O'Brien, plays by Edward Albee and especially *Cry The Beloved Country* by Alan Paton. William Golding's *The Inheritors*, *The Man Who Loved Children* by Christina Stead and *A History of Philosophy* a very waterstained (it was probably piss) edition of Mervyn Peake's *Titus Groan*, lots of bad science fiction and some good stuff by Bob Shaw and Moorcock's Sword and Sorcery stuff which I really blazed throughout. I found the worlds I read about incredibly alien and I found reading awful difficult what with the need for concentration and the big words you didn't understand. But I remember this sudden, overpowering emotion one boring afternoon at the end of the Paton book (about injustice in South Africa) and the shock of how much it had moved me. I'm sure there were tears in the eye and the next thing I knew I was sniffing around the tragically understocked Menzies in town spending good money on bloody books! I remember my more-worried-than-usual parents brought me a Nietzsche boxed set for Xmas 1980! Very festive! Also Michael Moorcock's *Cornelius* trilogy was bought around then. Then I bought *The Outsider* by Camus and *The Immoralist* by Gide. Those two books left me in tatters and I haven't stopped reading since.

About a year later I started writing: terrible poems, ponderous lyrics for non-existent bands, watery philosophical ponderings. The idea that anyone else in Scotland was a writer didn't cross my mind for an instant because of the strange, international melée I was reading. The most contemporary Scottish book I'd read was Iain Crichton Smith's *Consider the Lilies*, which is a wonderful historical novel but it made any concept of a contemporary Scottish literature seem more distant. What a sense of alienation! That has never left me. I can't express how completely I believed there was nobody alive in Scotland writing a book and I can remember the deep shock and amazement Alasdair Gray's mighty *Lanark* hardback gave me when a bright friend who'd stayed on at school and been lent it by his English teacher, showed me a copy with its distinctive artwork. I couldn't afford to buy the book but on my record-buying train trips to Glasgow I did discover the 'Scottish literature' section in Smith's bookshop. *Morvern Callar* was begun in 1991 and written pretty quick. I was living in Edinburgh then, in a cold room, working on the railways with a mounting sense of despair about where my life was going. It's true that I phoned in sick some days so I could just write it and it's also true I couldn't afford Tippex on top of beer money so I used two layers of milk of magnesia! The manuscript sat in a shoebox for close on two years since I'd no confidence or courage or indeed practical knowledge to send it off somewhere. If I'd got indigestion I could always have swallowed a few pages.

**S. R.** What, if any, popular cultural influences are there on your writing style and content?

**A. W.** I think it is very difficult to even define what popular cultural influences are any more. I think there must be some insecurity in our writing generation if we think we must differentiate between what is popular culture of any particular historical period and what isn't. When Shakespeare puts Falstaff in The Boar's Head tavern is that a reference to popular culture? As I said earlier I find this obsession, in a lot of contemporary culture output, with dropping musical and fashion and trendy nightspot names pretty pointless. 'How is it relevant to the story?' is what we'd better be asking. Obviously, my characters in the three novels that have been published so far are living in the nineties surrounded, like all of us, by aspects of contemporary culture. I'm taking notes towards an historical novel, set in the early nineteenth century and what will the influence of contemporary culture be on that historical work? Zero of course, because it depends on *what* you're writing about how popular culture impinges on your content. Sometimes painfully, there has to be reference to 'aspects of popular culture' but I think critics and some readers often confuse a reference to some aspects of 'popular culture' as an endorsement of support for it; they assume it's being celebrated. *Morvern Callar* came to be looked on by some people as a sort of lifestyle tract in nightclub culture. Rather chillingly, a mate told me that on some internet chat site the other day he 'met' a young American girl who claimed she 'based her life on *Morvern Callar*'. It always seemed to me that my treatment of that so-called 'rave culture', especially in *These Demented Lands*, was pretty cynical. I think there is a clear mocking of the ephemerality of it. And that family tree of rock bands too in *These Demented Lands*. All the fashion and style mags that interviewed me when I was that week's thing didn't consider for a second I was actually attacking aspects of that culture. The way music and cassette lists were used in *Morvern Callar* is often commented on, but I saw those rather obsessive, prosaic catalogues as serving a very definite *dramatic* function in the narrative: Morvern is listening, not to *her* music but to the favourite music of her dead boyfriend, therefore that prescriptive, rather hysterical listing had an emotional point. I wasn't just dropping a load of fashionable song titles. Far from fashionable; the range of the music referred to was very wide, dare I say 'catholic' (or must I invoke Father Ted? More shortly). Stravinsky, Luciano Berio, Manuel De Falla, Pablo Casàls, Cathy Berberian, John McCormack, as well as post-Ornette Coleman guitarist James Blood Ulmer, were all mentioned but nobody at *The Face* was anxious to discuss that music, just the 'rave' connection. We could equally discuss the classical music (I prefer the term Orchestral) in *Morvern Callar*. Far from popular culture, I think some of that music could fairly be labelled 'unpopular culture' which I'm pretty sure has been more influence on me. While I don't see my work as celebrating popular culture I'm disturbed by the critical faculty who seem increasingly obsessed with that culture. I think there's a good chunk of wet liberal New Labour angst behind it all. 'I like crap, therefore I'm an ordinary person'. It reminds me of these condescending 'Polytechnic' deconstructions of soap operas that tell us the mythic dramas being played out in *EastEnders* or *Neighbours* are actually closely related to Sophoclean tragedy and the 'people' shouldn't feel guilty for watching them. Give me *Oedipus Rex* anyday. *The Sopranos* was reviewed in the *Scotsman* (it was more a profile of the author, demanding that I hurry up and kindly produce the masterpiece that is expected of me). That novel happens to feature five teenage school girls and a Catholic priest. In the course of that review, the critic, Jenny Turner, managed to mention the Spice Girls two or three times and *Father Ted* once. I was astonished those were the best intellectual references this critic could muster up. I think that's exceptionally lazy criticism, from someone who is watching too much telly, just bouncing around all these names of television and pop culture. You end up with this poverty-stricken, catchphrase criticism. 'Is Scot Lit the new Brit Pop?' was the best example I saw!

**S. R.**  What do you think of today's political culture? Does your fiction have any connection to it?

**A. W.**  My fiction so far has always had people with little money and power as central characters (Brotherhood and Father Ardlui being the obvious flipsides of that). I think my work is closely connected to political realities, at least as far as I understand them in the Scottish Highlands. In *Morvern Callar* there is Red Hanna, the disillusioned left-winger and trade unionist who retreats into the love of a woman but betrays her at the first opportunity with Morvern's teenage best pal. Like many of us, Red Hanna's retreat is from hope into hedonism. He's a main character in another novel I'm working on set amongst railwaymen in the 1980s and 1990s. In *The Sopranos* there's an obvious collusion between the ideology of the teenage schoolgirls and the moral emptiness of Father Ardlui and the submarine captain. These men who've sucked along with the system (military or religious) all their lives and really believe in nothing and stand for redundant concepts like the Cold War and a merciful God! *The Sopranos* are no angels, but in the end they refuse to lie for the priest. On a personal level I feel completely divorced from British 1990s mainstream politics and parties who don't have anything valid to offer people. Everyone just toes the line. All these petit bourgeois values have won out. Almost all politicians are corrupt, only interested in staying in power and privilege rather than holding any values. It's all about licking the arse of business and middle class tax payers, avoiding any political hot potatoes and flying around the world in First Class. Nineties politics has sunk to the insanity of Alasdair Darling having his beard shaved off to improve New Labour's 'image' while Tornados fly out to support an unofficial war, bombing children in Iraq. Of course in Scotland there is at least the novelty of the forthcoming parliament but I've been living in Ireland for a long time now. I'm an Irish resident and I'm distanced from the changes going on in Scotland. There are still people in communities and especially in certain grass roots section of the Trade Unions, fighting on a daily basis to improve the lot of workers who struggle near the breadline and it's those folk I feel closest to, and I'm still involved with, in various private ways. But on a personal level I can't deny it's been awkward for me. I don't work on the railway anymore. I'm self-employed, living in Ireland and I've been incredibly fortunate. The easy, monolithic targets of eighties politics – the police during the Miners' Strike, Thatcher, Murdoch, the South African Embassy – have gone now and with all the main pillars of the Tory years still enshrined in law and legislation, this disgraceful replacement Establishment has never been more powerful or well defended. I suppose a retreat into hopes for Scotland as a more caring, socially enlightened democracy with a revived Trade Unionism is my path, but bastards can wear kilts too.

I have a sense of despair about it all and I think that's reflected in the novel I'm working on at the moment. That novel is also about political invisibility across Europe as a whole. One main character is an economic immigrant from the sub-Sahara, one of the 50,000 men, women and children who risked their lives crossing the Straits of Gibraltar in makeshift patera boats last year to get to the promised land of mainland Europe. There are 150,000 'illegal' immigrants from North Africa and the sub-Sahara living and working for incredibly low wages in Spain just now, trying to head north into the Benelux countries and to the former eastern bloc. Theirs is 'an unwritten life' to quote Herman Melville.

*Irvine Welsh*

# Post-Punk Junk
Irvine Welsh

*Irvine Welsh was born in the late 1950s and grew up around Leith.
He is author of the novels* Trainspotting, Marabou Stork Nightmares,
Ecstasy *and* Filth *and the short stories* The Acid House. *His contributions
to anthologies are too numerous to mention. He has written two plays*
Headstate *and* You'll Have Had Your Hole.

*Irvine Welsh's contribution to DJ culture includes having his own 'band'
Hibee-Nation and the infamous collaboration with Primal Scream and
legendary dub producer Adrian Sherwood for Euro '96 'Big Man and the
Scream Team Meet The Barmy Army Uptown' as well as DJ'ing in clubs like
Basics in Leeds and Sankey's Soap in Manchester amongst many others.*

*Welsh's most famous work is probably always going to be*
Trainspotting. *It reached the last ten books for the Booker Prize.
The book was, appropriately, described as the 'voice of punk, grown
up, grown wiser and grown eloquent' according to the* Sunday Times.
Variety *dubbed it a 'Clockwork Orange for the 90s' when it was
committed to celluloid. In its various forms as a book, play, film and
club reading it has been taken as a cultural sign of the 'end of the
century'.* Trainspotting *is more accurately 'post-punk'. In an interview
included in John Hodge's screenplays for* Trainspotting *the film, Welsh
admitted that; 'If you're being pedantic about it, you could say that it
was set in Edinburgh between 1982 and 1988, but the issues of drug
addiction and drug abuse and the ongoing HIV issues are as pertinent
as ever – probably more so now'. Alex Usborne, the producer of*
The Acid House *movie which Welsh scripted, (having just missed
out on* Trainspotting*) regards Irvine Welsh's first two books as quite
simply 'masterpieces'. His most commercially successful novel* Filth *is
also being filmed. He has also written extensively for TV.*

*Irvine Welsh lives in London and Edinburgh. I talked with the 'Big
Man' during breaks in rehearsals at West Yorkshire Playhouse in Leeds
and in bars in Edinburgh. He also later faxed me answers to some
questions I still wanted to ask.*

**STEVE REDHEAD** What were your influences? What about the Beat Generation for instance?

**IRVINE WELSH** It's really hard to say. I never really got into Kerouac that much and Burroughs I was a bit iffy about as well you know. I was never a great reader of fiction, that's the problem that I had. People make the assumption that if you work in some medium a lot of your references come from that medium as well. I think the biggest practical influence I had was through working for the council. I had to write detailed committee reports and physically writing the lot in a short space of time was the most important thing I had to do. Even if it's a lot of shit just physically writing the lot, handwriting or word processing. But actual influences, I think it's more TV and film and obviously people around you. I never had role models. I wanted to like Kerouac and Burroughs more than I did, you know what I mean, because of the influence that they had. It's obviously kind of books like Hunter S. Thompson's *Hell's Angels*, that kind of work, that's a documentary one.

I think what the novel never really recovered from in Britain in the eighties was the media getting obsessed with power and all that – it still is – and to an extent you see that in all the stuff' about Julie Burchill's kind of thing. If you ask people, if you took a poll amongst journalists and asked who is more important in culture in the seventies and eighties, John Lydon or Julie Burchill, I bet you the journalists would probably say Julie Burchill. If you ask people outside in the street, outside of that world you know, it would be 'who is Julie Burchill?' Power becomes more concentrated. The media has become very much a kind of self-serving stagnant pool. So many writers are referenced in the media, you see the reference in the media when they write. I wanted to write about the parts that the media doesn't reach and has got absolutely no influence in. It's like people might read the *Record* or *Sun* or *Mirror* or something but it's got absolutely no real influence in their lives in any kind of meaningful way. There must be some sort of process of conditioning that goes on at the moment but it's 'the telly' or 'the football', that's as far as it goes.

**S. R.** Were you to some extent writing 'against' an image of the writer?

**I. W.** I had an idea of what I didn't want to be. I wasn't totally hostile to Burroughs and Kerouac but it's like with writers in Glasgow like James Kelman and Alasdair Gray that I really liked, I think I was writing against them as well. I've said too that I was kind of writing against Martin Amis. But I've only read *London Fields* and that was the book that I reacted strongly to. I wanted to write against that kind of thing. I respect the fact that it's a really good book on certain levels. People will say 'oh he hates Martin Amis' and it's not like that at all. In fact in some ways he's very inspiring by providing that kind of thing. I used to get 'oh he hates James Kelman and all this stuff' and it's not that kind of thing at all. You're writing against, you're reacting against, what goes before to some extent.

**S. R.** *Trainspotting* was published eventually in the nineties but it was set much earlier presumably?

**I. W.** It started off as my diaries, what happened was that I got so fed up and de-motivated with my job and I just started writing these things up as fictions to amuse myself in the eighties. Then house music started with an urgency of its own, and I started to put a kind of creative tinge, I started to functionalise it, started to think about it and work in a creative sense. It kind of grew from there. I thought it was more a kind of keeping myself sane. I was jumping around in fields and clubs at weekends and then going back to the nine to five and it was a terrible come down. It was a way of keeping myself going, keeping things ticking over.

**S. R.** Secker and Warburg accepted the book in 1992 and it came out in 1993, is that right?

**I. W.** I finished it roughly about 1991 and I got encouraged to send it out. I showed it to one or two people. I sent a couple of stories out to wee magazines and they published them. Then it caught the eye of Duncan McLean basically and Duncan in some convoluted way managed to track me down and got in touch and I didn't realise there was all this stuff going on.

In the meantime I checked out Duncan's stuff and these magazines and saw that people were doing similar things to what I was doing. So it was weird to see all that kind of happening.

**S. R.** How did the publication of *Trainspotting* and the other books actually come about?

**I. W.** There was a message from a posh Scottish voice left on my ansaphone. I thought it was just one of my mates from the pub taking the piss so I left and went on holiday and when I came back there was another message saying 'can you please get in touch' and I just ignored it again and thought this guy's really persistent. I just couldn't work out who it could be, it could be a number of people. But what I did then was I got a letter from them confirming it saying 'please get in touch' and they said 'have you got somebody else publishing it?'. They published it and it sold quite moderately, a few thousand, but there was quite a wee buzz around it in Scotland. What happened next was I had the stories for *The Acid House*. I had *Trainspotting 2*, a sequel, which I've still got which I have never bothered to put out. I had this other stuff that I'd done, these stories, I put these stories in with the novella. They came out six months later which was very quick in publishing terms after the first one. It was actually, originally, *The Acid House* which was the one to do it, because of the title, the packaging. It started to sell. It outsold *Trainspotting* in the first period. Then the play came out of *Trainspotting* and that kind of kicked it off to another big high. It just went crazy. It started to rise up and the film obviously helped. It went mainstream. It probably shouldn't have happened. It is maybe not the kind of material that should go mainstream but it did.

**S. R.** How has *Trainspotting* changed your life?

**I. W.** I get asked to do appearances all over the world. The book is translated into everything, Japanese, Arabic, Yiddish, everything you can think of. Sitting opposite someone on the train reading the book is a kind of strange feeling. It's like an unsatisfying feeling because you want to know how they're sort of reacting to it. If you go and see a play or you go and see a film you can actually see people, it's a social thing, you see people kind of responding to it. And you feel increasingly detached from it the bigger it gets. It does get appropriated. At first it was my book. Then it was Danny's film. Then it was Ewan's film. And now it's even gone beyond that. When people say *Trainspotting* they think of Richard Branson. It's become that appropriated, it's right into the heart of consumerism now. That's the reason I didn't do *Trainspotting 2* then. I was going to do it after *Trainspotting*. I was going to do it after the first *Trainspotting* then I thought, nah, *The Acid House*. After that I got into writing *Marabou Storks* – it seemed a more interesting thing to do rather than retread. The time when it would have been right to do it would have been straight after the film.

**S. R.** The next novel *Ecstasy* was a much less satisfactory book than the other three despite its chiming with the MDMA influenced times in the mid-nineties in Britain which undoubtedly led to its commercial success. Has it made you more determined to stage a literary 'comeback'? What else have you done apart from your first play and publishing *Filth*?

**I. W.** I had to be a lot more careful with the book *Filth*. I feel a lot more confident as a result. I've taken a lot more care. And I know, I just get that feeling that it's back up to the standard of the first three. That's the way it panned out. But that would have been the time – after *Marabou Storks* – to do *Trainspotting 2* instead of *Ecstasy*. But since then I've had the idea that I want to rewrite it, five years ahead, the end of *Trainspotting*. I've always thought of it as a continuous thing. Whether I will or not I don't know.

They shot *The Acid House*. Three stories from it. Not the same producer/director. It's Paul McGuigan and Alex Usborne. We're gonna do *A Smart Cunt* as well – we're just doing the screenplay for that. A lot of the music from *The Acid House* film is good. We've got a couple of albums worth. About forty tracks. It's a mixture, all kinds of stuff. Oasis have done a track for it, The Chemical [Brother]s, Primal Scream. I've been more instrumental in getting people who I've got contacts with to do some stuff. I've not really had much input into the selection of the stuff. I think you can interfere too much.

For *Marabou Storks* I've had a couple of offers for the [film] rights but I've fought shy of them so far because I just don't like the idea that something should be made into a film because it's a book. I'd have to be really convinced that the people who were doing it were right. I don't know if it's appropriate to make that book into a film – it's a different medium. You have to think really carefully where these things get placed. I'd fight shy of that. I mean the play, *You'll Have Had Your*

*Hole*, people came round asking me if I wanted to make it into a film, even before it was performed – it's ridiculous. It's amazing that two of the stories in *Ecstasy*, the worst two, the first two, have been optioned as well so there's a chance that they'll hit the screen. Possibly for the better. It depends what relationships you forge. It obviously depends on your agenda. Sometimes it's what you want to be involved in. There's a *Disco Biscuits* film supposed to be coming out – 'The State of the Party' and two other stories, one of them is the Nicholas Blincoe story. They're going to be intertwined. The difference with *The Acid House* is that Alex Usborne wanted me to get involved by doing the screenplay. Fair enough, I'm quite into doing that. I'm doing other stuff as well. It just depends what you want to do.

**S. R.** How far is your fiction about the changing political culture of the last decade or so?

**I. W.** I think my writing is a response to the changes of the last ten years and how they affect working-class communities in general. When I look at the stuff of some writers that I admire, say Jimmy McGovern, one of the main themes is betrayal – unions, welfare state, churches, extended and nuclear families, how those institutions have failed the working-class by failing to protect them from global capitalism and the disintegrating society. I kind of take all that as given and I'm more interested in what the 'Thatcher's Children' generations of forty and under of the working class get up to – how they survive in the current economy and society.

**S. R.** You have written about soccer 'casuals' a lot in your fiction. What do you think about 'New Football'?

**I. W.** 'New Football' is essentially about redefining the supporter as a consumer. The 'new fan' is a 'celebrator' rather than a supporter, an active or passive cheerleader in a media fest. There's no real substance to the new footballing culture and technology and sponsorship/entertainment will eclipse sport. It's possible to see software packages replacing footballers and software designers replacing managers. That 'football' has little interest to me as it's a culture that is uniform and imposed from the top down. I think 'old football' will continue but it'll happen more off-camera. I think life is best lived off-camera and the most interesting things will always happen there.

**S. R.** You have railed against 'misleading' divisions like gender in your fiction and in your journalism. The media have attacked you on these grounds haven't they?

**I. W.** I feel the media have created an industry in inventing spurious divisions which are superficial. It's no longer to do with understanding complexity but with niche marketing. They thrive on creating false deficiencies so that they can sell products to make us more 'complete'.

**S. R.** Yet the media have to some extent put *Filth* back up there with *Trainspotting* ironically?

**I. W.** It's probably been, in some quarters it's been the best received since *Trainspotting*. In others it's been a kind of vindication of how depraved and perverted I am and all that kind of stuff so it's really what you expect now. What's happened is that it's polarised the critics to an extent. It's not really the shock of the new that *Trainspotting* had, it's not that kind of thing that's become a style icon that people feel they have to say they like even if they don't. It's actually getting treated as a proper book now. It's getting treated as 'proper' literature. It's basically getting critics to see their own sort of prejudices about the stuff that they like, whether they're for or against. I think it was a departure in a way. Because it's quite a strong book and has quite a strong personal identity it's given me a bit of distance from *Trainspotting* and all that cultural appropriation stuff that went along with it. The thing now is that it's been signed up by Miramax to be a film so I can see – given the way they want to do it – it's quite a commercial movie, quite a slick thing, quite 'hardcore' but done very glossy. I am quite happy for it to go ahead that way.

When I did *The Acid House* film I liked the idea that I could do something in my own way and make it hardcore and then somebody else could take it and they could do something with it and it might not be what I would have done but I wouldn't invalidate it or negate it because of that. It's interesting to see something that hits different parts of the whole spectrum. Things become appropriated so quickly now. You can become quite a radical force and a reactionary force at the same time just depending on where you're sitting, your glass being half empty or half full sort of thing. I wanted to get rid of all the 'Britpop' style wankers, I wanted to get back to doing something that was nasty again, that was edgy and pushing things further. My only regret now is that I killed off Bruce!

*Filth* was a difficult book to do because just like *Marabou Stork Nightmares* you have a character who is very difficult to live with, whatever you think of him. He's got this personality, he's a very hard character to live with. When you get somebody who's right out like that you can make comments about society, about power relationships, about authority. The Bruce character was not the classic authoritarian personality. The classic authoritarian personality is very servile to their bosses, and really fascistic to their subordinates whereas he is very manipulative and controlling to both, you know he hates his bosses and his subordinates equally, he is even handed, which is quite unusual for somebody in that position. Organisations tend to breed authoritarian personalities – it's their hierarchical nature. He's that kind of maverick. What I really hate is the idea that in the mainstream where the cops are the good guys, the Bruce Willis-type characters, they've always got to be this subversive slight character who doesn't go by the rules but all they're actually doing is saving the world from the 'Arabs' or the 'Communists' or aliens or whatever. They make the world safe for the suburbanites, so they're all respectable figures. So I wanted to take somebody who was a real reactionary, respectable figure doing the things that most authoritarian personalities do subconsciously, using his power in that organisation, very nakedly, very much in an aware way. It's somehow covering up for something, a spoiled idealism, that things should and can be better.

That's the kind of thing that I'm trying to get across in my writing now – there is no real opposition within the mainstream, the Labour Party has become the Tory Party because all the left have been kicked out of it, the unions don't have any power any more. Even the radicals and the churches, that side of religion, that's been blunted. So it's basically people who are outside the system that have got any sort of radicalism: you're either right outside society or you're exploited.

Say the people working in these direct line insurance places who are stuck in these little pods. It's very hard for people's own self-image, self-esteem, to admit that they are being exploited in some way so they've got to go along with this. So in the absence of any real political opposition all you've got is, there's no real tension or dynamic in the mainstream society, it's all these trivia, it's a collection of lists, like the internet, fashion, style. It's like a quest to find newer things and different things, more choices, more meaningless choices. What we really need is freedom *from* choice. You want a coffee, you don't want to stand there for hours saying Brazilian, Moroccan, you just want something wet! Too much of people's three score and ten is about making these meaningless choices, it's wasted on these completely meaningless choices. But there isn't any real political agenda to challenge that sort of capitalism. I think what you can really do is to make a nuisance of yourself, just to throw up the whole extremities, how it makes people, and how these people are both excluded from the system and are actually incorporating themselves right into the system. Sometimes I feel pretty bleak about it.

The book I'm doing now, I wanted to do a more upbeat, happier book after *Filth* but I'm writing all this nice positive stuff and I'm thinking well fucking hell I don't really believe it. I come back up here to Edinburgh and talking to my pals and people and everybody's getting shat on in so many different ways. You've got to represent that in what you're doing. You can't just write an upbeat book. The next one is really pissing me off because I wanted to do something positive and hopefully it will still have upbeat and hopeful elements in it but I just don't seem to do upbeat and hopeful very well. *Filth* has probably been the most successful book in terms of sales.

**S. R.** Do you think your personal success as a writer has made it more difficult for you to write about that politics and that culture?

**I. W.** Yeah, it's very difficult to know what the process is by which you do these things anyway. I think probably in a sense it's about being more comfortable now. It gives you more time to think about the injustices. It's that old story. If you're working nine to five you've not really got time to look. It is more external to me now. It's not intrinsic now. If I look back at the crap jobs I've had and sitting on the dole that's from memory now rather than a sort of feeling. The subtleties of the change as well; the sort of oppression is the same but the subtleties change from generation to generation. If you look at sexuality, it used to be this whole thing, the porn industry – it used to be this idea in the seventies that if somebody got paid off from a factory, they had this problem with sexuality – they couldn't get it up – but the next generation who have known nothing but the dole, it's completely different. Just shagging, shagging, shagging all the time, shagging and porn. It's actually the yuppies who are working all these long hours, have all this fatigue and don't have time to do that kind of thing, so that's switched around from the time in the eighties when all the middle-classes were enjoying sex and all that, and the working-classes' 'manhood' was more threatened. It's completely switched the other way now.

That's an area of interest I want to reflect in the writing next. It's just one of the changes, nobody's really noticed it, it's just talked about in terms of burn out and yuppie fatigue. But it's not, it's actually more to do with globalisation and casualisation. People who are in work have no time for anything else but work. They have no mental space to accommodate anything else but work. Whereas people who are outside the system will always find ways of amusing themselves. Even if they are materially disadvantaged they'll still find ways of coping, getting by and making their own entertainment. There's so much happening. If you come up to Edinburgh and go drinking with your mates and they tell you they've been sitting in a lock-out in the pub making porn movies and all that kind of stuff, you think to yourself well I don't really want to do that, I don't want to get my kit off and dive in and have pictures on the internet with my big white arse covered with pimples. You think to yourself I'm not really engaged in that kind of thing – if I had stayed up here in Edinburgh, if I'd stayed working, maybe I'd have just got into that kind of stuff. You wouldn't feel awkward and voyeuristic, rather than it would just be a natural thing being pissed at the end of the night and the security cameras on everybody.

**S. R.** Are there things you miss from the earlier days before you became famous?

**I. W.** There's a freedom, you've lost a freedom. It's people's expectations. I don't know what it is. Is it partly yourself being kind of snooty about where you started? I don't really think it is. It would be quite embarrassing to your friends if you started doing something like the *Visitors' Guide to Edinburgh* that I did with Kevin Williamson because it becomes an expectation of people around you, not so much that you're up there but you've achieved a certain place that demands that you behave with a bit more dignity. Things you haven't got a chance to get away with. It's a shame! It's like at the Hibs against Middlesbrough pre-season game in Edinburgh myself and Paul Reekie we'd been up all night doing speed, and we went straight to the game and as we were going out Paul was violently sick over this bouncer in the pub. At the match we did some pills at the game and I fell over outside the same pub and the guy went '2–0 to you boys!' You can get away with that within reason but the sense of abandon goes. You wake up the next day and you think 'fuck, I fell over outside the pub'. It's probably just a thing about getting older as well. You think to yourself maybe I shouldn't be behaving like this, I should be acting my age.

There is an inhibition, but it's not as much of an inhibition as people think. There's also a thing about the global media. You did something like the *Visitors' Guide* and nobody really gave a toss, a bit in Edinburgh, a few papers and all that. Everything went to the people you wanted it to go to. It wasn't designed to have some American Professor in the States looking over it. I think the only reason you watch what you say is today's *Observer* column is tomorrow's quote in the *Evening News*. When people you don't know start to take an interest in you it's an inhibiting thing.

**S. R.** What specific things in the media that have been levelled against you have you wanted to react against?

**I. W.** I don't think there's any point in reacting against it. It's almost like a buggin's turn-type cycle. It's something you have to ride out. You're not in a position of objective truth with the media, right and wrong. That's not what it's about. One thing that Kevin Williamson and I were discussing was we're probably going to get misrepresented and slagged off in the media but as long as we get the column inches

– that was the whole thing at first. Now you're selling books the column inches become a bit of a pain, they become intrusive and a bit boring. At the same time in the early days you play such a part in this self-mythologising process – men do that anyway – you pick one aspect of yourself and you pump it up and push it and it promotes that side of you. If you look at specific criticisms of either myself or the books I just think 'keep 'em coming'. If they stopped doing it I'd be a bit concerned. You shouldn't really expect to find any truth in it all, that's not what the media's for, it's not what it's for now. Particularly things like value-laden things like arts or entertainment or culture or whatever. The media's not really about truth at all. It's about opinion and prejudice basically. Maybe in some ways it should be.

**S. R.** One of the examples would be drug culture. Do you think it's had a negative or positive effect on your work?

**I. W.** It's very hard to say because it's hard to think how much you're influenced by the body of criticism, how that actually feeds into the process of what you do as a writer. I tend to ignore it. The first reviews I saw of *Filth* were the ones on the dust jacket, the new ones. You get sent them and the next copy comes out, the mass market copy, highlighting which ones would be best on the jacket. And that's the only purpose they've served for me. It's more you do get a feedback from people. You go out clubbing and all that. You go out to a pub or you go out to a football match and it's basically 'keep the drugs coming!' type of thing. It must have an influence. But I still hold to the idea that it's pretentious now to *not* write about drugs. To me they're just an unremarkable part of the scheme of things. When I see a novel that hasn't got any drugs in it I think to myself 'well, what kind of social life is this supposed to be depicting?' It's a subculture they're writing about.

**S. R.** Do you think the success has given you a platform to say what you want to say about these things, or is it all in the fiction?

**I. W.** Kevin Williamson in *Drugs and the Party Line* got a platform to do that. He's done that really well, he's been really comprehensive about that. In a sense I do keep my own views and the characters' views quite separate. It's not very interesting novelistically when things start to get too didactic, unless it's a character – a soapbox – who's like that. I've never confused these things. Obviously the drugs laws are stupid and irrational, they're a total mess, they're killing people. I would never come out and say that in a novel. I don't see it as the role of a novel. I just see it as more a value-free thing. Obviously if people are getting victimised or incarcerated or injured or killed by getting some dodgy gear through no quality control you've got to take all these issues into account when you're writing. If you read novels of rural Scotland, you can't write a novel about rural Scotland without describing the scenery, the mountains and the wild life and all that stuff. I don't think you can write a novel of urban Scotland without describing everything and drugs is integral to that; drugs are integral to social life.

The writing has given me things to do that are more expressly political like the Arthur Wharton thing – Britain's first black footballer – and the Liverpool Dockers thing – Jimmy McGovern and the Dockers Writing Group. But it's always got to work dramatically. I'm not really that interested in directly preaching about the politics. It's got to be shown dramatically. It's like the whole idea that in any society there's a society in conflict. Drama's all about conflict and choices and all that. So the two things are always going to be co-terminus. But it's more how it's done. In the *Dockers* thing one of the things Jimmy McGovern said – I would never have dared to say this, but he could get away with it, being a scouser – was that we've got to love the scabs. People who have been through all that with the Liverpool Dock strike, you could have heard a pin drop when he said that. I actually like writing characters that I don't feel empathetic towards. It's a struggle to get into that character, it makes it more interesting to try and work out what somebody who has got completely opposed viewpoints to you feels about things. I like people who have got really extreme, kind of guy-in-the-pub-type view, whether they're left, right or no politics at all, I just like that bombasticness. I was up the other night with my pals and a couple of guys that I grew up with in Muirhouse and we're just sitting having a drink and one guy has always played the devil's advocate, he always winds up this other guy who's really sincere and thinks about it. After all these years, thirty years, he still rises to the bait all the time. This guy switches from left to right and back across the spectrum.

**S. R.** You've been a DJ, and had a band Hibee-Nation, for quite a while now. Did that come from the writing success?

**I. W.** What happens is the more I got into the DJ-ing, the more I got into the music, the writing was taking a bit of a back seat. Which was good at the time because I was getting fed up. Then I thought well it's time to get into the writing again so the music and the DJ-ing started taking over. Before I first got the band together we said right from the start it was just going to be something that we would do as a kind of secondary interest – we've all got our own little day jobs in a way. When we do get together we enjoy it more, it's a kind of release from the other things. But what it does mean is that it becomes very difficult if everybody's busy, it's very rare that we've all got free time. We've done a new single which we're pleased about, and we've started to do some more tracks and finish an album. As for the DJ-ing, I tried to call a halt to it a little bit. I have done a lot of stuff over in San Francisco where a pal owns a pub and I think to myself I'm not a brilliant DJ, I'm not a fantastic mixer or anything like that – so you think 'what are you doing playing places like Manumission in Ibiza? You're keeping somebody out who is a fantastic DJ, you're just becoming a celebrity ponce'. So what I'm doing is much more kind of underground, small club, pub stuff. I'm much happier in that kind of environment. Most of the time in London. I'm happier with just a crowd of drunks coming in, and playing some old stuff and getting them all up. It is a fantastic buzz when you're playing somewhere like Manumission and you've got like six thousand people up and jumping away, but, you think, it's a holiday crowd and they're all pissed up and they're going to do it anyway whoever's on. But somebody who's really talented could be there if you're not in this slot. I've got a wee bit of a conscience about that in a way. I'll always do it because I enjoy it. One of the reasons I've come up here to Edinburgh to write this book is to basically get away from the decks in London. I just never get anything done. I always end up on the decks.

*Kevin Williamson*

# Rebel Rebel
## Kevin Williamson

Kevin Williamson was born in Kirkwall, Orkney, in the early 1960s. He started Rebel Inc as a literary fanzine ('litzine') in the early 1990s. He is author of Drugs and the Party Line and the editor of the collections of novellas, Children of Albion Rovers and Rovers Return. He has also contributed 'Heart of the Bass' to Disco Biscuits.

Rebel Inc magazine ran for five issues between 1992 and 1994. It was of major significance in the history of the underground literary press. It published new work by Irvine Welsh, Alan Warner, John King, Laura Hird, Toni Davidson and others before they had any books published, or were well known. Football (and music) fanzines of the 1970s and 1980s were also very much a source of inspiration for Rebel Inc. As Kevin Williamson says in the introduction to the Rebel Inc sampler Sampled: Writing from the Edge; 'fanzines. That was the thing. DIY. One man and his photocopier. Punk did that'. In 1993 Kevin Williamson was one of the first to organise crossover events which linked dance music and DJs to new fiction writing. Where Rebel Inc led many followed later in the 1990s.

Rebel Inc has been a book imprint of Canongate Books in Edinburgh since the mid-1990s. It specialises in publishing new – and good old – fiction. Rebel Inc books have published first novels by Laura Hird and Toni Davidson as well as reissuing underground classics. Rebel Inc now publish Charles Bukowski, Nelson Algren and Richard Brautigan among others. It has done much to resurrect Alex Trocchi who Irvine Welsh has described as 'the George Best of Scottish writing'.

In 1998 Kevin Williamson announced his candidacy for the new Scottish Parliament on behalf of the Scottish Socialist Party. In 1999 he fought a seat in Edinburgh where he lives. While he was away in Amsterdam researching a second edition of Drugs and the Party Line we e-mailed each other over several weeks.

**STEVE REDHEAD** How did fanzines influence you? Did they kick start *Rebel Inc?'*

**KEVIN WILLIAMSON** Fanzines have appealed to me since I was at school, going right back to *Sniffin Glue* and *Zig Zag* in 1977. They were writing about the only kind of music I was into back then – punk rock (even now I still hate the term new wave). The best fanzines, like the best of the punk music that spawned them, were political, angry, confrontational, in your face. These smudgy photocopied publications from the front line really fired up my imagination. It wasn't just the idea that they were independent, cheap and fast. Though that was definitely part of it. What really appealed was that anyone could do this, and by anybody I meant me. Right from the word go I saw fanzines as a participation thing rather than as something that was just bought or read.

I started one, called *Watership Down*, in 1978 when I was working at Dounreay. Ran them off on the Dounreay photocopier in between card schools and throwing buckets of nuclear waste into the sea. I seem to remember it had this sicko punk horror story in it that I wrote at the time (I was 17). I hope to fuck no one's still got a copy! Then in the eighties it was football fanzines. I loved them, couldn't read enough. I suppose my favourite one has been, and still is, *Not The View*, a Celtic fanzine. The writing is so sharp, intelligent and funny, and like in the spirit of all good fanzines it got involved, played a pivotal role in the campaign to oust the old Celtic board who almost put the club into receivership in 1994.

But it was *Cut* magazine in Scotland that was the gateway to *Rebel Inc*. This was a big distribution glossyish magazine that covered music, politics, books and cartoons. (Grant Morrison used to do this satirical Adolf Hitler cartoon that caused a bit of a ruckus at the time.) But the feel of it was pure fanzine. Then something weird happened. The magazine was doing great, a commercial success, but then in 1989, I think, it was bought over by an English publishing company who relocated it to London and it was never seen again. Conspiracy theories abounded. Still don't know what happened though. Anyway from then on I wanted to fill the gap left by *Cut*. I honestly thought I could do it. The next year I tried to put together a fanzine called *CASUAL-T* with this guy Niall Fulton, which was heavily influenced at the time, musically, by the Madchester thing. We planned out a whole issue but it never got off the ground. Funny thing was I never saw Niall until seven years later when he was starring as the writer Alexander Trocchi in a play, which, by a strange coincidence, I had written an intro for in the programme! Edinburgh is like that. It just goes round in circles. Anyway, after *CASUAL-T* stalled in the starting blocks I was editing an Edinburgh community newspaper, the *Tollcross Times*, which was wound up by the local authority because they didn't like my front page editorials criticising their general fecklessness at fighting the poll tax and urging people not to pay it. At this time I was also in touch with a writer called Duncan McLean who was doing photocopied booklets of short stories and poetry. I just loved that sense of immediacy that Duncan so enthusiastically championed with his *Clocktower Press* booklets and I decided there and then that I was gonna produce a glossy literary fanzine that tapped into what seemed to me like an explosion of streetwise young writers who were emerging in the east of Scotland at that time. I ran a short story competition with Gordon Legge and Duncan McLean in 1991 to get material and put out as many feelers as possible. We ended up, if that's the word, with Gordon Legge, Duncan McLean, Irvine Welsh, Barry Graham, Alison Kermack and others in the first issue of the magazine in May 1992, although prior to that *Rebel Inc* published two poetry booklets, one by Barry Graham and one of my own. Both of them were written in the same week that they went on sale. It was a really exciting time, a bit like the early days of punk it felt like to me. Everything was so fresh. I wanted *Rebel Inc* to be more than a magazine, to do one-off booklets, to do events with music, bands and later in clubs, with bits of sharp poetry and writing on T-shirts, flyposted onto bus stops, you name it, and that's exactly what happened. Anyway, the net kept widening with regards to the writers, and it still is, only now it has gone global, pulling in writers from every continent, a bit different from the tongue-in-cheek 'fuck the Glaswegians and the English' attitude that some of us had back then!

**S. R.** How did you get started as a fiction, non-fiction and poetry writer?

**K. W.** I've always enjoyed writing stuff down, stories and things, and I suppose I started my first (unfinished) book at about 14, second year at High School. I've honestly never thought about this for twenty years or so, but I remember showing it to some of my mates and some of them joined in with the book, suggesting bits. Funny thing was, it was written in a broad Thurso accent, taking the piss a bit, and now when I think about it, you know, it was really just a take on the stuff done at the time by the comedian Billy Connolly. At that time in the mid-seventies Connolly was a story-telling genius. Now he's become a bit of a Hollywood luvvie but back then he was an iconaclast, a rebel, and I honestly believe, and I've never heard anyone else say this, it was Billy Connolly who paved the way for James Kelman and the whole explosion of Scottish writers who followed. Connolly was attacked by the church; he was attacked for swearing, for his use of language, but he used the Glasgow street banter and dialect to construct these long rambling surreal monologues about working in the shipyards, going to the football, and just everyday life for working-class Glaswegians. I regard Connolly (as he was back then) as up there with Lenny Bruce and Bill Hicks as one of the all-time comic geniuses. Not a joke-teller but a story-teller. Of course, Connolly came out of the folk music circuit where story-telling was part of the whole thing. Folk music ain't my cup of tea in general but a good story-teller is still a good story-teller.

**S. R.** What other influences were there?

**K. W.** Back then it wasn't writers so much as song-writers who were the real influences. Particularly David Bowie. Those space-age lyrics and weird images. That's what turned me on. Marc Bolan too. And Lou Reed. And then later, after the whole punk thing which turned me inside out, it was people like John Lydon, John Foxx, Mark E. Smith, Ian Curtis. I thought these guys were the real poets not the shite I'd read in school because they were dealing with ideas and images which just seemed to make a connection at the time.

I'm trying to think of the books I read back then too and it was stuff like Richard Allen's *Skinhead* books, Timothy Lea's *Confession* books, the *Edge* books [violent westerns], Mario Puzo's *The Godfather*, the Hell's Angels books such as *Chopper and Mama*, and Dennis

Wheatley's black magic and satanist books. Real pulp novels, sex and violence a-plenty, which were passed surreptitiously around the school playground probably much the same as *Trainspotting* and *The Football Factory* are today. I seem to remember reading about seventy Agatha Christie books in a row for some strange reason and I don't think I worked out the murderer in any of them.

Then came sci-fi. Nothing but sci-fi for years. And this was the strange thing. I'd been filling my head with Robert Heinlein, Asimov, EE Doc Smith, whatever, and I got for my 21st birthday a copy of Alasdair Gray's *Lanark* which I thought was a sci-fi novel. Fucking loved it. It changed everything for me. This was imagination in free flow. It was like Ziggy Stardust with a social conscience and a sense of humour. But best of all, near the end of *Lanark* is an Index of Plagiarisms. It's got a list of all the bits from other books that Gray pillaged, lifted and reworked (or post-modernist intertextuality, as nicking other people's stuff is more properly called nowadays). I thought that was a really funny idea of Alasdair Gray's. Taking the piss and doffing the cap at the same time. Anyway, I tried to read all the writers in Gray's Index (there are loads) and that's how I first came across Camus, Sartre, Dostoevsky and loads of others. But most importantly for me was checking out James Kelman's short story collection *Not Not While The Giro*. Gray had included all of Kelman's short story 'Acid' in his Index, a story which I thought was like a masterpiece in miniature. Still do. A story that is only one paragraph long about someone who has fallen into a vat of industrial acid. Kelman was the business. You can't underestimate his influence. Like with Billy Connolly in particular, but also Tom Leonard, Peter MacDougall and other Glaswegian writers of the time, he helped give ordinary Scottish people a confidence boost because he actively championed the use of the Scots language as it was spoken and made a lot of people think about the way *our* language was being marginalised to make way for someone else's. It was like the penny finally dropped. This was during the Miners' Strike so a lot of pennies were starting to drop then. I was on the dole at the time, ducking and diving, in a bedsit sleeping and reading all day, listening to music, then drinking, playing pool, card schools all night, bookie shops, football, usual sort of stuff – fucking great it was too, better than working any day – and here was a writer not only writing about all of this but in a language that was real to me. After that, I started writing with a bit more sense of purpose, thinking about language and dialect. But it was years before I showed any of this to anyone. Writing poetry or stories wasn't something you owned up to, it wasn't really part of the culture I was in. Or so I thought at the time.

**S. R.** This culture was being legally and socially regulated in the late eighties and nineties in such a way that the content of certain fiction, poetry (and indeed some non-fiction) reflected the history of state surveillance. Were you aware that this was what was happening?

**K. W.** This gets right to the heart of so many things. History? I'd have to say that nowadays the official version of history is no longer recorded in books but in newspapers and current affairs television. This is where bits of truth, opinion and fiction are repeated so often that they merge and become the New History. Books are reduced in this way to 'alternative opinions' and their authors wheeled out merely as foils for official spokespersons in televised debates etc. Recently, I've ended up myself being assigned that role in quite a few debates on the drug laws. It's a a good rule of thumb that the more in conflict with authority the events were as they happened then the more likely they are to be rewritten later to suit the authorities. A recent example was the downfall of Margaret Thatcher. Read the papers or listen to political commentators on TV and you'd think she'd been felled by a speech by her ex-Chancellor Geoffrey Howe, or through a by-election defeat, rather than a colossal rebellion against an unfair tax that involved millions, included breaking the law on an unprecedented level, which saw riots in towns all over Britain and saw the centre of London go up in smoke at one of the biggest demonstrations post-war Britain has ever seen. While a few honest reports of this popular rebellion appeared at the time in a few of the less conservative broadsheets even they have long since been turned into fish and chip paper and have been buried under the New History of the time.

Another example, in a similar vein, is when you hear of the events that took place in France 1968 described almost universally as a student protest. May 1968 in France was in reality the biggest political earthquake ever to hit Western Europe and at one stage had ten million workers simultaneously on strike, occupying their places of work, and teetering on the precipice of revolution. Student protest? Aye, right. But see how easy it's done. Keep repeating that mantra of fiction in the mass media and it is eventually accepted into the canon of popular history. Road protests, the women of Greenham Common, the Miners' Strike of 1984–5, drug culture and most youth and music-driven cultures are treated likeways. The actual events and the truth are distorted to fit in with official thinking. You can probably see what I'm getting at when it comes to what has motivated me as a writer and publisher. When I wrote *Drugs and the Party Line* it was specifically written to challenge the New History of how the drug laws came into being and of how successful government policy has been on tackling drug-related problems. This was non-fiction. Just as Matthew Collin did with his book *Altered State* on rave and dance culture. But other writers over the last ten years have used fiction to record what is in essence a social history, a history that has been written out of official New History. Take Irvine Welsh's writing. *Trainspotting* isn't an official record of events in Muirhouse and Leith in the mid-late eighties. It's fiction. Yet it tells the story of what it was really like for some people at that time, people who are now officially reduced to mere AIDS fatality statistics, yesterday's unemployment statistics, or whatever.

Similarly, in *Marabou Stork Nightmares* another kind of fictionalised version of history was being recorded about the Hearts takeover of Hibs and the phenomenon of Hibs football casuals. These are not included in the official version of Edinburgh Life In The Late Twentieth Century as perpetuated by the local media etc. if you see what I mean. But AIDS, mass unemployment, the rise of the Hibs football casuals, the Hearts takeover, the closure of the docks, ecstasy and dance culture, these were events that affected working-class people in Edinburgh much more so than anything that ever happened in the festival or when Edinburgh hosted the European summit or the vote for a Mickey Mouse Parliament.

I guess it was left to writers to fill the vacuum and fiction seemed to be as good a way of doing this as anything. It is worth noting that the best of the Scottish writers who have made an impact in recent years are predominantly from working-class backgrounds and/or politically left of centre. Novelists like Irvine Welsh, James Kelman, Alasdair Gray, Iain Banks, Alan Warner, Martin Millar, Gordon Legge, Laura Hird, Duncan McLean, Janice Galloway, Alan Spence, James Meek, William McIlvanney, AL Kennedy, Barry Graham, in fact the list goes on and on. Not a Conservative among them and not a Blairite either to my knowledge. And then there's the poets, screenwriters and playwrights. A coincidence? I don't think so. Yet between them we have a body of work that is much more authentic as a real history of the time than the official version dealing mainly with politicians, general elections, royalty and such like. I suppose as a writer I've tried to be part of that without actually making any conscious decision to do so. Rebellion in every form and at every level is the natural order in an unjust society and is an integral part of the culture we live in. Just like with publishing, as a writer you try to be faithful to that culture, do it justice.

**S. R.** What is the future for *Rebel Inc* and the 'literary underground gone overground'?

**K. W.** It has to go forward I suppose, or be left behind. I suspect that after the hedonistic excesses of the late eighties and nineties, the next period will be more reflective, more critical, less superficially cool, and maybe the words agit and prop will once more come together with a new dynamism, in tune with a general post-millennial looking forward. I kinda suspect that uncool concerns such as the environment, diminishing fuel supplies, quality of food, and health, will take on a new lease of life as people try and work out where the hell we are going and what kind of world do we want to have for our kids. A lot of people all over the globe are gonna see this fucking great void lying ahead which is gonna have to be filled with something. Throw in an economic recession or two and the bubble of social calm is gonna burst and then things could get quite interesting. Could be a rough ride for a lot of folk.

I'll be trying as much as possible to keep *Rebel Inc* in touch with developments as they unfold, fermenting ideas, locking horns with the mainstream when necessary, remaining '*engage*' as Sartre called it. I'd like to see a new engaged and loosely organised movement emerge in the near future that embraces all the threads of the radical counter-cultural in art, music, theatre, writing and politics. And become a force to be reckoned with. I'd like to see such an underground movement able to respond quickly to events and lend weight and support to such disparate things as workers in dispute (like the Liverpool Dockers were recently) as well as taking on the repressive drug laws and things like unnecessary new roads or genetic modifying of food. I can't help but think that writers like John Pilger, Irvine Welsh, and the playwright Jimmy McGovern, as well as Chumbawamba and Robbie Fowler, did so much to publicise the Liverpool Dockers' dispute and that this kind of thing could become much more organised and less reacting on the spot to events. I mean, the time is ripe. Who would have predicted a few years ago that while Noel Gallagher sipped champagne with Tony Blair at Number 10, Damon Albarn would be out on the streets with students protesting against New Labour's education policies? I suspect that Albarn is more in tune with what lies around the corner. There are loose parallels with 1967 and 1968 when the summer of love, peace, sex and drugs turned into a full-scale global rebellion against – fuck – everything. By 1968 there was the anti-Vietnam war movement, race riots, Stonewall, radical feminism, even revolution on the streets of Paris and Prague. Personally, I'd settle for a good healthy mix of both '67 and '68!

As far as publishing goes I'm gonna keep putting out-of-print counter-culture and underground texts back into circulation as well as scouring the globe for new stuff. A lot of writers are really pushing themselves now, trying to innovate, provoke and stimulate. Grappling with big ideas and keeping it new and relevant. I think this will continue, even more so.

My next book will either be fiction or non-fiction or poetry. Definitely. One of the three. Seriously, I'm working on all three but in no great hurry to finish. I'm also planning to update and expand *Drugs and the Party Line*. But first – I think I'm gonna be working with my old mate Wes on a film script of *Scream 3*.

# Chronology

| | |
|---|---|
| 1993 | Jeff Noon *Vurt* |
| | Irvine Welsh |
| | *Trainspotting* |

| 1993 | Jeff Noon *Vurt* | 'Back To Basics' for Tories |
|---|---|---|
| | Irvine Welsh | *Rebel Inc Invisible Insurrection* |
| | *Trainspotting* | night |
| 1994 | First *Pulp Faction* anthology | Criminal Justice and Public Order Act |
| | | Oasis *Definitely Maybe* |
| | | USA '94 |
| 1995 | Alan Warner *Morvern Callar* | Leah Betts Ecstasy death |
| | Nicholas Blincoe *Acid Casuals* | Leftfield *Leftism* |
| | Emer Martin *Breakfast in Babylon* | |
| 1996 | *Trainspotting* the movie | Underworld 'Born Slippy' rereleased |
| | John King *The Football Factory* | IRA bombs in London and Manchester |
| | | Euro '96 |
| | | Drum'n'Bass |
| 1997 | Sarah Champion *Disco Biscuits* | Blair wins election |
| | Mike McCormack *Getting It in the Head* | Hacienda closes |
| 1998 | *The Acid House* the movie | Scottish and Welsh 'devolution' referenda |
| | | Irish 'peace' agreement |
| | | France '98 |
| 1999 | Toni Davidson *Scar Culture* | Ethnic cleansing in Kosovo |
| | *Britpulp* anthology | NATO bombs Yugoslavia |
| | | Chemical Brothers *Surrender* |

# The Guide

All of the fiction and playscripts by the authors interviewed in this book are included in this guide, as well as fiction by related writers. Read on!

Ambrose, Joe (1998) *Serious Time: A Rap Diary*. London: Pulp Books.

Ambrose, Joe (1999) *Too Much Too Soon*. London: Pulp Books.

Antoine, Patsy (ed.) (1999) *Afrobeat*. London: Pulp Books.

Atkins, AD (1995) *Ecstasy, Sorted and On One*. London: Atkins.

Barlay, Nick (1997) *Curvylovebox*. London: 20/20.

Beard, Steve (1999) *Digital Leatherette*. Brighton: Codex.

Blincoe, Nicholas (1995) *Acid Casuals*. London: Serpent's Tail.

Blincoe, Nicholas (1997) *Jello Salad*. London: Serpent's Tail.

Blincoe, Nicholas (1998a) *Manchester Slingback*. London: Picador.

Blincoe, Nicholas (1998b) *My Mother Was A Bankrobber*. London: Revolver.

Blincoe, Nicholas (1999) *The Dope Priest*. London: Sceptre.

Bower, Mick (1998) *Football Seasons*. London: Pulp Books.

Bracewell, Michael (1988a) *The Crypto-Amnesia Club*. London: Serpent's Tail.

Bracewell, Michael (1988b) *Missing Margate*. London: Minerva.

Bracewell, Michael (1989) *Divine Concepts of Physical Beauty*. London: Minerva.

Bracewell, Michael (1992) *The Conclave*. London: Secker and Warburg.

Bracewell, Michael (1995) *Saint Rachel*. London: Jonathan Cape.

Brook, Jonathan (1994) *Slackness*. London: Backstreets.

Brook, Jonathan (1995a) *Big UP!* London: Backstreets.

Brook, Jonathan (1995b) *Herbsman*. London: Backstreets.

Campbell, Sheri (1997) *Rude Gal*. London: X Press.

Champion, Sarah (ed.) (1997) *Disco Biscuits*. London: Sceptre.

Champion, Sarah (ed.) (1998) *Disco 2000*. London: Sceptre.

Champion, Sarah and Scannell, Donal (eds) (1998) *Shenanigans: An Anthology of Fresh Irish Fiction*. London: Sceptre.

Champion, Sarah (ed.) (1999) *Fortune Hotel*. London: Penguin.

Cooper, Dennis (1992a) *Frisk*. London: Serpent's Tail.

Cooper, Dennis (1992b) *Wrong*. London: Serpent's Tail.

Cooper, Dennis (1994) *Closer*. London: Serpent's Tail.

Cooper, Dennis (1995) *Try*. London: Serpent's Tail.

Cooper, Dennis (1998) *Guide*. London: Serpent's Tail.

Corrigan, Susan (ed.) (1997) *Typical Girls*. London: Sceptre.

Coupland, Douglas (1991) *Generation X: Tales for an Accelerated Culture*. New York: St Martin's Press.

Coupland, Douglas (1992) *Shampoo Planet*. New York: Simon and Schuster.

Coupland, Douglas (1994) *Life After God*. New York: Simon and Schuster.

Coupland, Douglas (1995) *Microserfs*. London: Flamingo.

Coupland, Douglas (1996) *Polaroids From The Dead*. London: Flamingo.

Coupland, Douglas (1998) *Girlfriend In A Coma*, London: Flamingo.

Craven, Bruce (1993) *Fast Sofa*. New York: William Morrow.

Crump, Simon (1997) *My Elvis Blackout*. Edinburgh: Clocktower Press.

Davies, Pete (1987) *The Last Election*. London: Penguin.

Davidson, Toni (ed.) (1989) *And Thus Will I Freely Sing*. Edinburgh: Polygon.

Davidson, Toni (ed.) (1998) *Intoxication: An Anthology of Stimulant-based Writing*. London: Serpent's Tail.

Davidson, Toni (1999) *Scar Culture*. Edinburgh: Rebel Inc.

Davidson, Toni (2000) *Wild Justice*. Edinburgh: Rebel Inc.

Doyle, Roddy (1988) *The Commitments*. London: Heinemann.

Doyle, Roddy (1990) *The Snapper*. London: Secker and Warburg.

Doyle, Roddy (1991) *The Van*. London: Secker and Warburg.

Doyle, Roddy (1992) *Brownbread* and *War*. (Playscripts) London: Minerva.

Doyle, Roddy (1993) *Paddy Clarke Ha Ha Ha*. London: Secker and Warburg.

Doyle, Roddy (1996) *The Woman Who Walked Into Doors*. London: Secker and Warburg.

Doyle, Roddy (1999) *A Star Called Henry*. London: Jonathan Cape.

Dyer, Geoff (1990) *The Colour of Memory*. London: Vintage.

Dyer, Geoff (1998) *Paris Trance*. London: Abacus.

Easton Ellis, Bret (1991) *American Psycho*. London: Picador.

Easton Ellis, Bret (1998) *Glamorama*. London: Picador.

Etchells, Tim (1999) *Endland Stories*. London: Pulp Books.

Fingers, Two (1995) *Junglist*. London: Backstreets.

Fingers, Two (1996) *Bass Instinct*. London: Backstreets.

Garland, Alex (1996) *The Beach*. London: Penguin.

Garland, Alex (1998) *The Tesseract*. London: Penguin.

Gentry, Alistair (1997) *Their Heads are Anonymous*. London: Pulp Books.

Gentry, Alistair (1999) *Monkey Boys*. London: Pulp Books.

Geraghty, Christine (1996) *Raise Your Hands*. London: Backstreets.

Girolamo, Emilia di (1999) *Freaky*. London: Pulp Books.

Gomez, Jerry (1996) *Our Noise*. London: Penguin.

Gomez, Jeff (1997) *Geniuses of Crack*. New York: Simon and Schuster.

Graham, Barry (1989) *Of Darkness and Light*. London: Bloomsbury.

Graham, Barry (1992) *Get Out As Fast As You Can*. London: Bloomsbury.

Graham, Barry (1995) *The Book of Man*. London: Serpent's Tail.

Graham, Barry (1997) *Before*. New York: Incommunicado.

Hartnett, P-P (1996) *Call Me*. London: Pulp Books.

Hartnett, P-P (1997) *I Want To Fuck You*. London: Pulp Books.

Hartnett, P-P (1999) *Mmmm Yeah*. London: Pulp Books.

Hawes, James (1996) *A White Merc With Fins*. London: Vintage.

Hawes, James (1997) *Rancid Aluminium*. London: Vintage.

Headley, Victor (1992) *Yardie*. London: X Press.

Headley, Victor (1993) *Excess*. London: X Press.

Headley, Victor (1994) *Yush!* London: X Press.

Headley, Victor (1995) *Fetish*. London: X Press.

Headley, Victor (1997) *Here Comes the Bride*. London: X Press.

Headley, Victor (1999) *The Best Man*. London: X Press.

Hewitt, Paolo (1995) *Heaven's Promise*. London: Heavenly.

Hird, Laura (1997) *Nail, and other stories*. Edinburgh: Rebel Inc.

Hird, Laura (1999) *Born Free*. Edinburgh: Rebel Inc.

Hollinghurst, Alan (1998) *The Spell*. London: Chatto and Windus.

Home, Stewart (ed.) (1998) *Suspect Device: Hard Edged Fiction*. London: Serpent's Tail.

Inyama, Ijeoma (1997) *Sistas on a Vibe*. London: X Press.

Indiana, Gary (1993) *Gone Tomorrow*. London: Hodder and Stoughton.

Indiana, Gary (1994) *Rent Boy*. London: Serpent's Tail.

Janowitz, Tama (1992) *The Male Cross-Dresser Support Group*. London: Picador.

Kureishi, Hanif (1995) *The Black Album*. London: Faber and Faber.

Kureishi, Hanif (1997) *Love in a Blue Time*. London: Faber and Faber.

Kureishi, Hanif (1998) *Intimacy*. London: Faber and Faber.

Lake, Kirk (1997) *Never Hit The Ground*. London: Pulp Books.

LeFanu, Sarah (ed.) (1997) *Sex, Drugs, Rock'n'Roll: Stories to End the Century*. London: Serpent's Tail.

Legge, Gordon (1989) *The Shoe*. Edinburgh: Polygon.

Legge, Gordon (1991) *In Between Talking About the Football*. Edinburgh: Polygon.

Legge, Gordon (1994) *I Love Me (Who Do You Love?)* Edinburgh: Polygon.

Legge, Gordon (1998) *Near Neighbours*. Edinburgh: Polygon.

Lewis, Simon (1998) *Go*. London: Pulp Books.

Liksom, Rosa (1993) *One Night Stands*. London: Serpent's Tail.

Linklater, Richard (1992) *Slacker*. New York: St Martin's Press.

Litt, Toby (1997a) *Beatniks*. London: Secker and Warburg.

Litt, Toby (1997b) *Adventures in Capitalism*. London: Minerva.

Martin, Emer (1995) *Breakfast In Babylon*. Dublin: Wolfhound.

Martin, Emer (1999) *More Bread Or I'll Appear*. New York: Houghton Mifflin.

McGrath, Melanie (1998) *Hard, Soft and Wet*. London: Flamingo.

McCormack, Mike (1997) *Getting It in the Head*. London: Jonathan Cape.

McCormack, Mike (1998) *Crowe's Requiem*. London: Jonathan Cape.

McLean, Duncan (1993) *Bucket of Tongues*. London: Secker and Warburg.

McLean, Duncan (1995) *Blackden*. London: Secker and Warburg.

McLean, Duncan (1996) *Bunker Man*. London: Vintage.

McLean, Duncan (1997) *Lone Star Swing*. London: Jonathan Cape.

McLean, Duncan (ed.) (1997) *Ahead Of Its Time: A Clocktower Press Anthology*. London: Jonathan Cape.

McLean, Duncan (1999) *Plays One*. London: Methuen.

Millar, Martin (1992) *The Good Fairies of New York*. London: Fourth Estate.

Millar, Martin (1994) *Dreams of Sex and Stage Diving*. London: Fourth Estate.

Millar, Martin (1998) *Love and Peace With Melody Paradise*. London: Prolesec.

Miller, Trevor (1989) *Trip City*. London: Avernus.

Newland, Courttia (1997) *The Scholar: A West Side Story*. London: Abacus.

Newland, Courttia (1999) *Society Within*. London: Abacus.

Noon, Jeff (1993) *Vurt*. Manchester: Ringpull.

Noon, Jeff (1995) *Pollen*. Manchester: Ringpull.

Noon, Jeff (1996) *Automated Alice*. London: Doubleday.

Noon, Jeff (1997) *Nymphomation*. London: Doubleday.

Noon, Jeff (1998) *Pixel Juice*. London: Doubleday.

Noon, Jeff (2000a) *Needle In the Groove*. London: Doubleday.

Noon, Jeff (2000b) *Cobralingus*.

Owen, Jane (1997) *Camden Girls*. London: Penguin.

Page, Ra (1999) (ed.) *The City Life Book of Manchester Short Stories*. London: Penguin.

Palmer, Elaine (ed.) (1995) *TechnoPagan*. London: Pulp Faction.

Palmer, Elaine (ed.) (1996) *The Living Room*. London: Pulp Faction.

Palmer, Elaine, (ed.) (1999) *Girlboy*. London: Pulp Books.

Q (1997): *Deadmeat*. London: Sceptre.

Ravenhill, Mark (1996) *Shopping and Fxxking*. (Playscript) London: Minerva.

Richards, Ben (1996) *Throwing The House Out of the Window*. London: Headline Review.

River, Michael (ed.) (1997) *Allnighter*. London: Pulp Faction.

Rushkoff, Douglas (1997) *The Ecstasy Club*. London: Sceptre.

Sampson, Kevin (1998a) *Awaydays*. London: Jonathan Cape.

Sampson, Kevin (1998b) *Extra Time*. London: Yellow Jersey.

Sampson, Kevin (1999) *Powder*. London: Jonathan Cape.

Smith, Karline (1995) *Moss Side Massive*. London: X Press.

Stewart, Sophie (1999) *Sharking*. London: Transworld.

Tillman, Lynne (1998) *No Lease on Life*. London: Secker and Warburg.

Warner, Alan (1996) *Morvern Callar*. London: Jonathan Cape.

Warner, Alan (1997) *These Demented Lands*. London: Jonathan Cape.

Warner, Alan (1998) *The Sopranos*. London: Jonathan Cape.

Waugh, Mark (1997) *Come*. London: Pulp Books.

Welsh, Irvine (1993) *Trainspotting*. London: Minerva.

Welsh, Irvine (1994) *The Acid House*. London: Jonathan Cape.

Welsh, Irvine (1995) *Marabou Stork Nightmares*. London: Vintage.

Welsh, Irvine (1996a) *Trainspotting and Headstate*. (Playscripts) London: Minerva.

Welsh, Irvine (1996b) *Ecstasy*. London: Jonathan Cape.

Welsh, Irvine (1998a) *You'll Have Had Your Hole*. (Playscript) London: Minerva.

Welsh, Irvine (1998b) *Filth*. London: Jonathan Cape.

Welsh, Irvine (1999) *The Acid House*. (Playscript) London: Minerva.

Welsh, Irvine and Williamson, Kevin (1993) *A Visitor's Guide to Edinburgh*. Edinburgh: Rebel Inc.

White, Tony (ed.) (1999) *Britpulp*. London: Sceptre.

Williams, John (1997) *Faithless*. London: Serpent's Tail.

Williams, John (1999) *Five Pubs, Two Bars and a Nightclub*. London: Bloomsbury.

Williamson, Kevin (1997) *Drugs and the Party Line*. Edinburgh: Rebel Inc.

Williamson, Kevin (ed.) (1996) *Children of Albion Rovers*. Edinburgh: Rebel Inc.

Williamson, Kevin (ed.) (1998) *Rovers Return*. Edinburgh: Rebel Inc.

# In the Background

Non-fiction background material to the interviews in this book is contained in this list.

Annesley, James (1998) *Blank Fictions: Consumerism, Culture and the Contemporary American Novel*. London: Pluto Press.

Bracewell, Michael (1997) *England Is Mine: Pop Life in Albion from Wilde to Goldie*. London: Harper Collins.

Bussman, Jane (1998) *Once in a Lifetime: The Crazy Days of Acid House and Afterwards*. London: Virgin.

Calcutt, Andrew and Shephard, Richard (1998) *Cult Fiction: A Reader's Guide*. London: Prion.

Campbell, Allan (1997) *A Life In Pieces: Reflections on Alexander Trocchi*. Edinburgh: Rebel Inc.

Cannon, David (1994) *Generation X and the New Work Ethic*. London: Demos.

Caveney, Graham (1998) *The 'Priest', They Called Him: The Life and Legacy of William S. Burroughs*. London: Bloomsbury.

Cohen, Jason and Krugman, Michael (1994) *Generation Ecch*. New York: Simon and Schuster.

Collin, Matthew (1997) *Altered State: The Story of Ecstasy Culture and Acid House*. London: Serpent's Tail.

Duncombe, Stephen (1997) *Notes From Underground: 'Zines and the Politics of Alternative Culture*. London: Verso.

Dunn, Sarah (1994) *The Official Slacker Handbook*. London: Abacus.

Garrett, Sheryl (1998) *Adventures in Wonderland*. London: Headline.

Greenfield, Karl Taro (1994) *Speed Tribes: Children of the Japanese Bubble*. London: Boxtree.

Hamblett, Charles and Deverson, Jane (1964) *Generation X*. London: Tandem Books.

Harrison, Melissa (1997) *High Society*. London: Piatkus.

Hodge, John (1996) *Trainspotting and Shallow Grave*. London: Faber.

Howe, Neil and Strauss, Bill (1993) *13th Gen: Abort, Retry, Ignore, Fail?* New York: Vintage.

Joseph, Jennifer and Taplin, Lisa (eds) (1994) *Signs of Life: Channel-Surfing Through 90s Culture*. San Francisco: Manic d Press.

Kadrey, Richard (1993) *Covert Culture: Sourcebook*. New York: St Martin's Press.

Kadrey, Richard (1994) *Covert Culture: Sourcebook 2.0*. New York: St Martin's Press.

Kennedy, Pagan (1994) *Platforms: A Microwaved Cultural Chronicle of the 1970s*. New York: St Martin's Press.

King, Martin and Knight, Martin (1999a), introduction by John King. *Hoolifan: Thirty Years of Hurt*. Edinburgh: Mainstream.

King, Martin and Knight, Martin (1999b), introduction by Irvine Welsh. *The Naughty Nineties: Football's Coming Home*. Edinburgh: Mainstream.

Kroker, Arthur and Kroker, Marilouise (1996) *Hacking the Future*. Montreal: New World Perspectives.

Leary, Timothy (1994) *Chaos and Cyberculture*. Berkeley: Ronin.

Linklater, Richard et al (1994) *Dazed and Confused*. New York: St Martin's Press.

McCaffrey, Larry (ed.) (1995) *After Yesterday's Crash: An Avant-Pop Anthology*. London: Penguin.

McKay, George (1996) *Senseless Acts of Beauty*. London: Verso.

McKay, George (1998) *DIY Culture*. London: Verso.

Miller, Jayne (1995) *VoXpop: The New Generation X Speaks*. London: Virgin.

Mulgan, Geoff (1997a) *Life After Politics: New Thinking for the Twenty-First Century*. London: Fontana.

Mulgan, Geoff (1997b) *Connexity: How We Should Live in the Twenty-First Century*. London: Chatto and Windus.

Perryman, Mark (ed.) (1996) *The Blair Agenda*. London: Lawrence and Wishart.

Perryman, Mark and Coddington, Anne (eds) (1998) *The Moderniser's Dilemma*. London: Lawrence and Wishart.

Reynolds, Simon (1996) 'Review of Trainspotting' in *Artforum* Summer.

Reynolds, Simon (1998) *Energy Flash*. London: Picador.

Rucker, Rudy, Sirius, R.U., and Mu, Queen (1992) *Mondo 2000: A User's Guide to the New Edge*. San Francisco: Harper Collins.

Rushkoff, Douglas (ed.) (1994a) *The Gen X Reader*. New York: Ballantine Books.

Rushkoff, Douglas (1994b) *Cyberia: Life in the Trenches of Hyperspace.* San Francisco: Harper Collins.

Rushkoff, Douglas (1997) *Children of Chaos: Surviving the End of the World as We Know It.* London: Harper and Collins.

Sharma, Sanjay, Hutnyk, John and Sharma, Ashwani (eds) (1996) *Dis-Orienting Rhythms.* London: Zed Books.

Sounes, Howard (1998) *Charles Bukowski: Locked in the Arms of a Crazy Life.* Edinburgh: Rebel Inc.

Taylor, DJ (1994) *After The War: The Novel and England Since 1945.* London: Flamingo.

Turner, Steve (1996) *Angelheaded Hipster.* London: Bloomsbury.

Vasili, Phil (1998), foreword by Irvine Welsh. *The First Black Footballer: Arthur Wharton 1865–1930: An Absence of Memory.* London: Frank Cass.

Welsh, Irvine (1998) 'Interview With Dennis Cooper' in *Dazed And Confused* Summer.

Wexler, Michael and Hulme, John (1994) *Voices of the Xiled: A Generation Speaks for Itself.* New York. Doubleday.

Wilkinson, Helen (1994) *No Turning Back: Generations and the Genderquake.* London: Demos.

Young, Elizabeth and Caveney, Graham (1992) *Shopping in Space.* London: Serpent's Tail.

Started in 1992 by **Kevin Williamson**, with help from established young authors **Duncan McLean** and **Gordon Legge**, Rebel Inc magazine set out with the intention of promoting and publishing what was seen then as a new wave of young urban Scottish writers who were kicking back against the literary mainstream. The Rebel Inc imprint is a development of the magazine ethos, publishing accessible as well as challenging texts aimed at extending the domain of counter-culture literature.

## Rebel Inc Fiction

**Children of Albion Rovers** £5.99 pbk
Welsh, Warner, Legge, Meek, Hird, Reekie
'a fistful of Caledonian classics' **Loaded**

**Rovers Return** £8.99 pbk
Bourdain, King, Martin, Meek, Hird, Legge
'Pacy, punchy, state of the era' **ID**

**Beam Me Up, Scotty** Michael Guinzburg £6.99 pbk
'Riveting to the last page . . . Violent, funny and furious' **The Observer**

**Fup** Jim Dodge £7.99 hbk
'an extraordinary little book . . . as good as writing gets' **Literary Review**

**Nail and Other Stories** Laura Hird £6.99 pbk
'confirms the flowering of a wonderfully versatile imagination on the literary horizon'
**Independent on Sunday**

**Kill Kill Faster Faster** Joel Rose £6.99 pbk
'A modern urban masterpiece' **Irvine Welsh**

**The Sinaloa Story** Barry Gifford £6.99 pbk
'Gifford cuts through to the heart of what makes a good novel readable and entertaining' **Elmore Leonard**

**The Wild Life of Sailor and Lula** Barry Gifford £8.99 pbk
'Gifford is all the proof that the world will ever need that a writer who listens with his heart is capable of telling anyone's story' **Armistead Maupin**

**My Brother's Gun** Ray Loriga £6.99 pbk
'A fascinating cross between Marguerite Duras and Jim Thompson'
**Pedro Almodovar**

# Rebel Inc Non-Fiction

**A Life in Pieces** Campbell/Niel £10.99 pbk
'Trocchi's self-fragmented lives and works are graphically recalled in this sensitively orchestrated miscellany' **The Sunday Times**

**The Drinkers' Guide to the Middle East** Will Lawson £5.99 pbk
'Acerbic and opinionated . . . it provides a surprisingly perceptive and practical guide for travellers who want to live a little without causing a diplomatic incident' **The Guardian**

**Locked In the Arms of a Crazy Life: A Biography of Charles Bukowski** Howard Sounes £16.99 hbk
'wonderful . . . this is the first serious and thorough Bukowski biography. An excellent book about a remarkable man' **Time Out**

**Drugs and the Party Line** Kevin Williamson £5.99 pbk
'essential reading for Blair, his Czar, and the rest of us' **The Face**

# Rebel Inc Classics

**1 Hunger** Knut Hamsun £6.99 pbk
with an introduction by Duncan McLean
'Hunger is the crux of Hamsun's claims to mastery. This is the classic novel of humiliation, even beyond Dostoevsky' **George Steiner** in **The Observer**

**2 Young Adam** Alexander Trocchi £6.99 pbk
'Everyone should read Young Adam' **TLS**

**3 The Blind Owl** Sadegh Hedayat £6.99 pbk
with an introduction by Alan Warner
'One of the most extraordinary books I've ever read. Chilling and beautiful' **The Guardian**

**4 Helen & Desire** Alexander Trocchi £6.99 pbk
with an introduction by Edwin Morgan
'a spicily pornographic tale . . . enhanced by an elegant and intelligent introduction by Edwin Morgan' **The Scotsman**

**5 Revenge of the Lawn** Richard Brautigan £6.99 pbk
'His style and wit transmit so much energy that energy itself becomes the message, Brautigan makes all the senses breathe. Only a hedonist could cram so much life onto a single page' **Newsweek**

**Stone Junction** Jim Dodge £6.99 pbk
with an introduction by Thomas Pynchon
'Reading *Stone Junction* is like being at a non-stop party in celebration of everything that matters' **Thomas Pynchon**

**7   The Man with the Golden Arm** Nelson Algren £7.99 pbk
'This is a man writing and you should not read it if you cannot take a punch . . .
Mr Algren can hit with both hands and move around and he will kill you if you
are not awfully careful . . .' **Ernest Hemingway**

**8   Snowblind** Robert Sabbag £6.99 pbk
with an introduction by Howard Marks
'A flat-out ballbuster, it moves like a threshing machine with a full tank of ether.
This guy Sabbag is a whip-song writer' **Hunter S. Thompson**

**9   Sombrero Fallout** Richard Brautigan £6.99 pbk
'Playful and serious, hilarious and melancholy, profound and absurd . . . how
delightfully unique a prose writer Brautigan is' **TLS**

**10   Not Fade Away** Jim Dodge £6.99 pbk
'a book which screams off the starting blocks and just keeps accelerating'
**Uncut Magazine**

**11   Ask the Dust** John Fante £6.99 pbk
with an introduction by Charles Bukowski
'a tough and beautifully realised tale . . . affecting, powerful and poignant stuff'
**Time Out**

**12   The Star Rover** Jack London £6.99 pbk
with introductions by Hugh Collins and T. C. Campbell
'an astonishing achievement' **The Sunday Times**

**13   A Walk on the Wild Side** Nelson Algren £6.99 pbk
with an introduction by Russell Banks
'Mr Algren, boy you are good' **Ernest Hemingway**

**14   Ringolevio** Emmett Grogan £7.99 pbk
with an introduction by Peter Coyote. Published June 1999

**15   The Iron Heel** Jack London £6.99 pbk
with an introduction by Leon Trotsky. Published June 1999

FOR YOUR FREE REBEL INC CLASSICS SAMPLER PLEASE CALL OR WRITE TO
CANONGATE BOOKS AT THE ADDRESS BELOW.

All of the above titles are available in good bookshops,
or can be ordered directly from:

**Canongate Books**, 14 High Street, Edinburgh EH1 1TE
Tel 0131 557 5111 Fax 0131 557 5211
email info@canongate.co.uk
http://www.canongate.co.uk